Making $50 a Week to Selling Millions

Unlock Your Inner Salesperson

John S. Ferguson

Table of Contents

Introduction:
From Timeshare Phones to Boardrooms—Your Sales Journey Begins

My first sales job was at a timeshare company, setting appointments over the phone for people to come to Laguna Hills or Glendale, California, and listen to a three-hour sales pitch. The company hired lots of young people with energy—it was all new to me! No sales techniques were taught. Just a simple pitch, and we were told to dial the numbers and deliver it.

The place had 25–30 reps setting appointments in one room. It was loud, and I could barely hear my customers. They played music at full volume while everyone talked over each other. It felt like a typical boiler room—young people, older people, gang bangers, just a rough crowd.

When I started making phone calls, I was timid and scared. I didn't have any sales experience, and I don't think I even needed any to get hired. I'd never had a sales job before this one. Since the place was so loud, I started crawling under my desk just so I could hear. That worked for a while until I decided to try a different approach—I'd get louder.

So, I stood on my desk and started delivering the pitch really loudly. I got louder than the people around me. I noticed that the louder I got, the quieter they all became. I think they were wondering what I was doing. They looked at me like I was crazy.

This was the first place where I started in sales, and I didn't even know it at the time. It was a rough place to work, but after I started getting louder, I noticed my excitement was increasing with every call. All of a sudden, my appointment count was going up. Everyone else was setting 5–7 appointments a day with a low show rate. I started setting 20 appointments a day with a higher show rate.

Once someone showed up for the three-hour sales pitch, I got paid an extra $25 commission. I realized it's a numbers game—the more appointments I set, the more likely someone would show up. The other appointment setters didn't have the energy and excitement I had. I used that to my advantage and quickly became the top appointment setter in the room. I was able to carry this experience with me to my other sales jobs, and I'm still teaching these methods today.

That experience taught me sales is about connection, hustle, creativity, and the courage to put yourself out there—even when you're standing on a desk in a chaotic room full of strangers who think you've lost your mind.

Your origin story might be different—trading cards, a family business, or a late discovery of sales entirely. Perhaps you're driven by curiosity, necessity, or simply by a desire to improve your persuasion skills. Regardless of where you started, if you're reading this, something draws you to sales. We all begin somewhere, and every journey brings questions, doubts, and those small victories that confirm we're on the right path.

This book exists to help you uncover the confident sales professional already within you. Whether you're new to sales or a veteran feeling something's missing, this is your roadmap. We'll journey from square one—where sales seems intimidating—to a place where you own your confidence, resilience, and leadership abilities.

Sales transcends smooth talk and memorized scripts. It's about understanding people, building authentic relationships, navigating challenges, and growing through adversity. If you've questioned whether you have what it takes, here's the truth: you absolutely do. No magical "sales gene" required—just the right tools, mindset, and willingness to learn, adapt, and show up authentically. This book delivers all three.

Why I Wrote This Book

I wrote *Making $50 a Week to Selling Millions* to share my journey and inspire you that anything is possible with dedication. Too often, I see salespeople quit before they give themselves a real chance—I call this "giving up before the miracle happens."

Early in my career, after receiving two commission checks totaling $50 before taxes (about $35 take-home), I faced a critical decision. Most people would have quit and moved on. But my mindset wasn't about wanting to quit—it was about refusing to accept $50 per week and figuring out how to earn more. The bottom line? It was my own doing. I simply needed to work harder for better results.

My mentor told me, "The pat on the back is your own paycheck." You must dedicate yourself completely, absorb everything like a sponge, and fully engage. Develop a mindset of learning everything about your job. Another piece of advice stuck with me: "Act like a lifer"—whether you're there one year or ten. When you act like this is all you have, you become the best at what you do. If you always have something to fall back on, you'll always keep one foot out the door. I had nothing to fall back on, so I had no choice but to excel.

Looking back while writing this book, I'm amazed at what I endured to reach where I am today. You must be willing to sacrifice, and when things go wrong, you must persevere and work through it. Reading this book and understanding the mindset required to be a great salesperson will elevate your success year after year.

Real-World Wisdom, Not Theory

Throughout these pages, you'll find practical, jargon-free techniques applicable immediately, regardless of experience level. We'll cover mastering fundamentals, sharpening communication, transforming objections into opportunities, and developing success-building habits.

Beyond tactics, I'll share timeless mindsets fueling growth in your career and life. Since sales success intertwines with leadership, we'll explore how to become someone others respect and trust—whether leading a team or working independently.

The path isn't always smooth. When I started cold-calling, I froze at every hang-up. Rejection felt deeply personal, and I nearly quit repeatedly. But each setback taught valuable lessons. That mentor's advice—"Every 'no' brings you closer to a 'yes'"—reframed challenges as stepping stones. Through feedback, practice, and honest reflection, I learned to bounce back stronger. Those awkward calls, difficult customers, and hard-won lessons shaped the salesperson, leader, and mentor I am today.

My career has spanned main street shops to corporate boardrooms, mentoring eager newcomers and coaching seasoned professionals facing burnout. I've worked with scrappy startups, established corporations, and passionate entrepreneurs. There's no universal script for sales greatness, but there is a proven process for revealing your best. This book offers actionable advice from real-world trenches—lessons learned, mistakes made, successes celebrated.

The Journey Ahead

This book follows the natural arc of a successful sales career—step by step, building momentum progressively.

We begin by exploring where sales careers truly start, connecting your unique history to future ambitions. Next, we examine the foundational traits that distinguish great salespeople: authenticity, empathy, grit, and curiosity. These aren't innate; they're muscles you strengthen.

Core skills come next—connecting with people, listening deeply, asking powerful questions, and communicating value with clarity and integrity. Then we tackle objections—the dreaded aspect that actually holds tremendous growth potential. You'll learn frameworks and real examples to turn "I'm not interested" into "Tell me more."

With basics secured, we shift to mindset—how your thinking shapes everything. We'll explore attitudes and rituals breeding resilience, adaptability, and long-term success. You'll discover how to project confidence and create magnetism, naturally attracting clients and colleagues.

Each chapter builds upon the last, creating a rock-solid foundation. By the end, you'll possess a complete toolkit plus the insight, perspective, and self-belief to keep growing beyond the final page.

Your Invitation

Bring your whole self to this journey. Whether seeking new tactics, deeper meaning, or proof that sales mastery is achievable, you're in the right place. Don't worry about feeling unprepared—every professional started as a beginner. All that matters is your willingness to take the next step.

Your transformation starts now. Let's unlock your untapped potential together and master the art and science of sales.

Dive into Chapter 1 with energy and an open mind—discover just how far you can go.

Chapter 1:
Learning to Survive, Finding My Way at 15

My journey really began when I moved to California from Oklahoma at 13 years old. Life wasn't easy back then. My parents had divorced and gone their separate ways, and my mom decided to move to California with her new husband so we could start fresh. At that age, getting a job was the furthest thing from my mind.

When I entered junior high, I didn't get much guidance from my parents. Now that I have my own son, I understand how important it is to help kids stay on top of their homework and build a sense of accomplishment. My grades suffered because nobody was holding me accountable. I remember how different things were when I lived with my dad in Oklahoma—he was much stricter about schoolwork. As a Vietnam veteran who'd done two tours and worked as an Oklahoma City police officer, he made sure I got my work done.

I wasn't always the best-behaved kid, which is probably why I was sent back to Oklahoma to spend a summer with my grandmother. Looking back, I think my mom hoped Grandma could get me back on track. And she did. My grandma was one tough woman who didn't take crap from anyone. She drove an 18-wheeler cross-country and owned her own bar. She even had a wolf as a pet at one point, and she loved animals so much that she kept geese, dogs, a pet raccoon, and even fed the skunks bread at night. We'd sit on the porch drinking sweet iced tea, waiting for the animals to arrive so we could feed them day-old bread.

Did I mention my grandma had worked as a deputy sheriff? She was tough as nails but sweet as peaches. I loved her so much. She taught me to be strong while still respecting people. I'm grateful my mom sent me there. I learned so much from her at a time when I really needed it.

High School Years

I returned to California with a fresh attitude and entered high school. Looking back, I was pretty much on my own during those years. If I wanted to do my homework, I did. If I didn't, nobody pushed me. My mom decided to move to a different city, which meant changing schools and getting to know a whole new set of kids. It wasn't easy, but I made new friends and even dated my first girlfriend during freshman year. All in all, it was a great part of my life—though I still hadn't given any thought to getting a job or building a career.

A Turning Point

When I turned 15, I was living with my mom in Fullerton, California, in a business park. My stepdad had converted his small warehouse into a two-story building with stairs and an upper floor for us to live in. My younger brother was only two years old. But something was missing for me.

By then, I was attending special education classes because I'd missed so much school and fallen behind. School wasn't a priority at the time. I often wonder now why I didn't take it more seriously. Looking back, I can see that I didn't have anyone holding me accountable—making sure I went to school, did my homework, and attended events.

In my special ed class, my teacher, Miss Jenny Bobo, became an inspiration. I started looking at her as a mother figure. She helped me with my schoolwork and encouraged me to be better. I remember her telling me I was going to be someone special when I grew up. Those words have stayed with me to this day. I believed her, and I wasn't going to disappoint her. Since I was somewhat of an artist, I drew her a clown-like cartoon figure with the word "bobo" and gave it to her, hoping she'd keep it and remember me as life went on.

On My Own

One day after returning home from school, I got into an argument with my mom. Since we were living at the business, she told me I had to leave and get a job, or I couldn't come back. This was hard for me. I'd never received any instruction on how to get a job or even do an interview.

That first night, I had nowhere to sleep, so I found a spot next to an electrical transformer in the business park. It was warm and made a buzzing sound, but at least it kept me from freezing. I tried to keep attending school, but it was incredibly difficult. I was in 10th grade and suddenly faced with finding work.

I put in a few applications and finally got a job at an ice cream shop. It was my first real job. Somehow, the conversation came up, and I mentioned to the manager that I had nowhere to sleep. She told the owner, who kindly invited me to stay at her house for a few nights until I found something more permanent. I was so grateful that someone reached out to me like that.

Her husband wasn't thrilled about me staying there, though. He told his wife I had to go. I guess he didn't want any freeloaders hanging around. By then, my mom understood that I'd found a way to be on my own, so I asked her to take me to the Social Security office to get my card for my new employer.

Working and Learning

I really enjoyed working at the ice cream shop and had fun with my coworkers. The pizza store next door became a regular hangout, and I quickly became friends with their employees. One night, they came over and asked if we could exchange ice cream for pizza. I thought it was a great idea since I needed to eat, but I didn't know how to make it work. The ice cream shop weighed everything that was wasted, and we had to record it all.

So, I came up with a plan. I'd "accidentally" drop a scoop or two on the side of the containers, then make shakes for the pizza shop employees without recording the waste. I did this for a few nights until I found out that even dropped scoops had to be recorded.

While working at the ice cream shop, I was also trying to go to school and work nights. It wasn't easy, and I started developing an "I don't care" attitude. I'd show up to school in the morning, skip first period, stop by the hamburger joint for breakfast, and often didn't arrive until second or third period.

Eventually, my mom got a call from the school about my absences and was called to meet with the principal. He told her I'd missed too much school and could no longer attend the regular high school. I'd have to go to a continuation school. I hated this idea because that school was for kids who'd gotten in serious trouble, been in juvenile hall, or even jail. I didn't want that, so I decided that since I was working, I didn't need school anyway. I never went back. I dropped out of high school in tenth grade.

Finding My Path

After working for a few months, I realized I needed to get back into education. I joined a regional occupational program that would let me earn my GED and possibly prepare for a career. I stayed in class for a few months, but I wasn't finishing my homework; it still wasn't my strong point. I had a strong will to work and wanted to find my way in the workforce. I'd discovered a new freedom and the ability to make money. For a while, I lived with my mom on and off.

My mom had been a stay-at-home mom for many years but took on a few jobs here and there when I was a kid. She didn't have much money, so it was difficult for her to take care of a teenager like me. I had to learn to be on my own at a very young age, and I had to learn fast.

I often look at my son now. As I write this, he's currently the same age I was when I had to be on my own. I realize how sad that situation was, but I also learned an important lesson: how to be a survivor.

A New Direction

Some friends told me about going to junior college to learn a skill that could help me get a job and build a career. So, I signed up, paid for my classes, and enrolled in a graphic arts program. I learned to run Heidelberg presses and AB Dick presses, figuring that if I did well, they'd help me find a job.

I graduated at the top of my class. The teacher really liked me and helped me get a job at a local printing company. I was feeling great about this new opportunity, but the store owner wasn't happy with my ability to keep up with the work. After just one day, he let me go.

Suddenly, I had no job. I wasn't working for the ice cream company anymore, either, so I needed to find another job fast.

I often looked back and wondered what it would've been like to graduate, go to prom, attend winter formals, and just be a normal part of high school. To this day, I regret not graduating from high school. But I also believe it was part of the plan all along. I believe there was a path I was supposed to follow, and this was it.

Chapter 2:
The Foundation of Sales Success

Most people think being a great salesperson means having a big personality, endless charm, and the ability to talk anyone into a deal. The truth? Those flashy traits are just surface-level. Real sales success isn't about showing off or pushing hard—it's about something more profound: mindset and habits that keep you going day after day, no matter what comes your way.

I learned this lesson long before I understood what sales actually was. At 16, I found myself standing outside a grocery store with 10 bottles of perfume, no training, no script, and absolutely no idea what I was doing. I just stood there silently, waiting for customers to notice me and ask what I was selling. Of course, no one did. People walked right past me as if I didn't exist.

In this chapter, I'll share what truly drives long-term success in sales—lessons I've learned from that awkward teenager fumbling with perfume bottles to the strategies that shaped my career. You'll discover why empathy, curiosity, resilience, and adaptability matter far more than charm.

What Really Makes a Great Salesperson

The image of the perfect salesperson still floats in many minds: an extrovert who dazzles with charm, always ready with a joke or a bold answer, never sweating a tough conversation. Yet sales history is crowded with quieter types—those who would rather listen than talk, who ask thoughtful questions rather than boast. True sales success comes less from charm and much more from qualities like empathy, genuine interest, resilience, and the ability to connect in authentic and ethical ways (DeCastro, 2020).

Standing outside that grocery store, frustrated and exhausted, I made a decision that changed everything. I walked across the street to an apartment complex and started knocking on doors. After several unanswered knocks, I approached one last door—and saw a big sign in the window: "NO SOLICITING."

But I was 16, tired, and determined. So, I knocked anyway.

Beyond Charm: The Power of Authenticity

A man swung the door open, already furious. "Kid, don't you see that sign? It says NO SOLICITING!"

I froze. My heart dropped. He was angry, and I was intimidated. I lowered my head, and for a split second, something came out of my mouth that surprised even me: "Sorry, sir... If I could read, I wouldn't be doing this job."

I turned and started to walk away. And just like that... everything changed.

His entire attitude shifted. "Wait—hold on," he called after me. "Are you serious? You can't read?"

I kept my act going. "Yes, sir... I'm sorry."

"Come back here," he said. "Let me see what you've got."

His wife came downstairs. He told her to take a look at the perfumes. She ended up buying all ten bottles on the spot.

The truth? I could read just fine. But I learned something priceless that day: Charm alone doesn't close deals. What closed that sale wasn't a rehearsed pitch or slick talking; it was an authentic emotional connection, even if manufactured in a moment of desperation.

Many might find the energetic, talkative salesperson entertaining, but entertainment doesn't always translate into trust or results. Some of the highest-performing sales professionals are actually introverts. They listen carefully, show patience, and tailor their approach to each customer.

Imagine two sales reps:

- The first dominates the conversation, tossing out rehearsed lines and crowding out the client's voice.

- The second asks, "How has your business changed this year?" and lets silence do its work.

The client begins to talk about challenges, the impact of recent changes, and hopes for the future. When the salesperson listens and asks, "What's the biggest frustration you face right now?" the conversation deepens. Authenticity—being real and present—outperforms surface-level charm every time.

That moment at the apartment door taught me something fundamental: people buy based on emotion, not logic. A split-second, emotionally intelligent response can completely flip anger into empathy. When you connect to someone's human side, they're more willing to help you. Sales isn't only about the product—it's about the story, the emotion, and the moment you create.

Empathy: The Foundation of Trust

Empathy is the foundation of trust in sales. It goes far beyond nodding mechanically or parroting back what the customer says. Active listening means tuning in to both words and tone. A good salesperson keeps quiet, pays attention, and avoids interrupting.

Looking back, even my clumsy teenage approach tapped into empathy. I (accidentally) made that angry man see me as a human being with a struggle, not just an annoying salesperson violating his clearly posted boundary. That shift in perspective opened the door to trust.

Nonverbal cues matter: folded arms, a sigh, or a quick glance away. Salespeople who pick up on these signals tailor their pitch on the fly. For example, if a client tenses up at the mention of a price, a good rep pauses and asks, "Is this number higher than you expected?" or "What concerns you about the cost?"

Genuine empathy means genuinely wanting to help, not just to sell. Here's a sketch of a dialogue:

- **Salesperson:** "Before we talk numbers, can I ask, what's most important about this purchase for you?"

- **Client:** "Honestly, I just want something that's going to last. I'm tired of products that break."

- **Salesperson:** "I hear you. Reliability really matters, especially when time is tight. Can you tell me about a recent experience where a product let you down?"

Such questions move the conversation from generic selling to personal understanding, leading to better solutions and trust.

Curiosity: The Strongest Tool

Curiosity is one of the strongest tools a salesperson can use. Instead of rattling off product features, curious sales professionals dig deep, asking thoughtful discovery questions:

- "What led you to look for something new?"

- "Can you walk me through a day where this solution might help?"

- "How have your needs changed this year?"

This mindset keeps sellers from making assumptions and ensures solutions fit actual needs. Curiosity leads to unexpected discoveries: a hidden pain point, a key decision-maker who went unnoticed, or a budget issue that calls for creative thinking. The most insightful salespeople learn more by asking questions than by giving answers, transforming discovery calls into real partnerships (DeCastro, 2020).

If I'd been more curious at 16—if I'd asked those apartment dwellers what scents they liked or what occasions they needed perfume for—I might have sold even more effectively than my improvised emotional appeal.

Resilience: Processing Rejection Productively

Resilience is a daily necessity for anyone in sales. Rejection happens all the time, and setbacks are part of the job. The difference between those who last and those who burn out is how they process these disappointments.

I experienced this firsthand while selling perfume. Standing outside that grocery store, getting ignored by dozens of people, I could have packed up and gone home defeated. Instead, I got frustrated—and that frustration pushed me to try something different. I walked to the apartment complex. I knocked on doors that didn't answer. And yes, I even knocked on a door with a "NO SOLICITING" sign.

A resilient salesperson faces "no" as information, not as failure. They review what happened—*Did I miss a need? Did I talk too much?*—then adjust for the next call. Some keep a notebook, writing a quick summary of tough calls and noting what worked or what to change. After a rough week, they might take a quiet walk, book a talk with a mentor, or switch up their routine to refocus.

Turning setbacks into learning moments keeps morale steady. Recovery isn't about ignoring tough feelings. It's about responding productively, whether that means reviewing wins to remember success or moving quickly to a new opportunity.

Influence Through Trust

Influence grows out of trust. This starts with honesty. Saying "I don't know, but I'll find out for you," earns more respect than pretending to know everything. Trust-building requires small, steady actions: showing up on time, following through, and treating people as partners, not targets.

Ethical persuasion steers clear of pressure tactics. Instead, it's about connecting solutions to real customer needs while being clear about limitations. For example, "This package fits most of your requirements, but I want to check that last detail with our engineering team before you commit," tells the customer they matter more than closing the deal.

Now, was my perfume story ethical? Honestly, probably not. I lied to close a sale. But what I learned from that experience—the power of emotional connection, the importance of reading people, and the ability to pivot quickly—became the foundation for building genuine trust throughout my career. I just learned to apply them honestly.

These traits—empathy, curiosity, resilience, influence—lay the foundation for solid sales habits. They shape discipline, how salespeople follow up, how they prepare, and how they build a client network for the long haul. The strongest sales behaviors all start from these core qualities, setting the stage for genuine success (DeCastro, 2020).

Attributes You Must Possess

Empathy, curiosity, and influence each rely on a powerful foundation of self-discipline, consistency, courage, and adaptability. For example, to listen empathetically every day, you need the self-discipline to focus on customers, not just during one great meeting but in every call. When you let curiosity lead a discovery conversation, consistency helps you ask thoughtful follow-up questions, even when distracted or behind on quota. Influence often involves trying new approaches on the fly—adaptability lets you shift gears and connect with all kinds of people.

That teenage version of me stumbling through perfume sales? I had adaptability in spades. I pivoted from grocery store to apartment complex, then from silent waiting to door-knocking. What I lacked was self-discipline and consistency. I didn't have a system or routine. I was just winging it.

Let me share the four cornerstone attributes you need, plus a simple, practical way to assess and improve them.

Self-Discipline

A top salesperson manages their day with the kind of discipline you see in elite athletes. The strongest reps carve out time each morning to review their pipeline, check follow-ups, and prepare for a full day, even when they'd rather sleep in or are tempted by distractions.

Imagine someone like Maya, who blocks off an hour before the office opens to send prospecting emails. She tracks outbound calls, meetings scheduled, and research completed, marking each win in her CRM. It's tempting to procrastinate on the tough calls or skip the planning, but Maya keeps herself honest with a daily checklist. Her peers may say she's "lucky" with her results, but it's her discipline that creates that luck.

Consistency

When high-performing salespeople are at their best, you see steady call volumes, follow-ups, and positive customer touchpoints. Consistency means showing up with the same quality, no matter what's going on elsewhere in your life.

Take someone like Ahmed, who gets the same review from every customer: "He always follows through." If Ahmed hits a rough patch outside work, his sales effort doesn't dip. This steadiness makes his pipeline reliable, and customers trust him. It's easy to be enthusiastic on good days—but your edge builds when you grind through the tougher ones, too.

Courage

Sales brings rejection, tough negotiations, and prospects who want to say no. Courage keeps you dialing when three people in a row hang up, or when you call a C-level leader who seems out of reach.

Think of Jessica, who always picks up the phone for those "impossible" accounts. Once, she called the head of procurement at a company known for saying no to all new vendors. She got turned down twice that month, but on the third try, her persistence and honest tone landed a meeting. Instead of giving up, she checks her emotions, resets, and tries again.

I learned about courage standing in front of that door with the "NO SOLICITING" sign. My heart was pounding. I knew I shouldn't knock. But something inside me said, "You're already here. What's the worst that can happen?" That split-second decision to knock anyway— that was courage. And while the outcome was fortunate, the real lesson was that courage often means doing the uncomfortable thing despite your fear.

Adaptability

No two sales meetings are the same. Customers you thought loved your pitch might react differently, or a new competitor could rewrite the conversation. Adaptable sellers shift tactics easily. When a discovery meeting veers off the agenda, you can listen, sense what's needed, and adjust.

For instance, Ben started one meeting with a financial controller ready to talk numbers, but the client needed to vent about a supply problem. Ben put aside his proposal, listened, then reframed the solution to highlight reliability and support. That flexibility closed the deal.

My perfume experience was all about adaptability. When standing silently didn't work, I moved locations. When knocking on doors got no response, I kept trying. When I faced an angry man, I instinctively adjusted my approach in real time. That quick emotional response— whether you call it resourcefulness or desperation—demonstrated the power of reading a situation and pivoting instantly.

Self-Assessment Framework

To really own these attributes, create a four-column grid with each attribute at the top. After each week, rate yourself from 1 (low) to 5 (strong) on each. For low scores, jot two reasons why, and one experiment to try next week. With high scores, write a strategy for maximizing that strength. Ask yourself honestly:

- *Where did I stand out?*

- *Where did I coast?*

- *Which habit can I add or tweak tomorrow?*

Self-discipline, consistency, courage, and adaptability—working together—set the stage for daily habits that drive wins. Your strongest routines flow from discipline; your best energy comes from being flexible. When you weave these attributes into every day, the routines and habits needed for high sales performance start to feel automatic, and your results reflect it.

The Disciplines You Need

Great salespeople turn reliable habits into daily rituals that drive their results. Skills like discipline, focus, and self-direction show up in routines that make high performance automatic.

Looking back at my 16-year-old self, I had none of this structure. I was reactive, opportunistic, operating on instinct alone. It worked once, but it wasn't sustainable. Real success requires systems.

Time Blocking for Peak Performance

Start by using time blocks to organize the day. Top performers break their days into focused work sprints and clear recovery windows, often using early mornings for prospecting or strategic calls when energy is highest.

For instance, Bill Creelman built Spindrift's early momentum by dedicating his most productive morning hours to contacting new accounts and solving supply challenges, before shifting to team meetings in the afternoon when his creative energy waned (BevNET Live L.A., 2025).

Strategic Energy Management

Pinpoint your three daily energy peaks, then match your hardest sales activities to these slots. Prospecting, pipeline review, and closing calls demand full attention, so schedule these during your most alert periods. Tasks like email clean-up or administrative work fit better during lower-energy stretches.

Integrate blocks for relationship-building and follow-up just after lunch, when direct selling may feel more draining. Chris Lansing's approach at Health-Ade involved dividing her day this way, using her afternoon dip for one-on-one coaching and operational reviews, which require a steady pace but less immediate creativity (BevNET Live L.A., 2025).

Tracking Systems That Drive Accountability

Systems for tracking metrics make disciplined routines stick. A daily success sheet drives clarity—create a simple grid on paper or an app. List activities like prospecting calls, follow-up emails, demos set, and deals closed. Jot down targets for each and fill in progress as you go. At day's end, total each column and reflect: Did you hit your numbers? If not, make a quick adjustment plan for tomorrow.

Bob Nakasone's teams at KeVita and First Bev adopted real-time tracking dashboards, so everyone could see where they stood on goals and self-correct quickly (BevNET Live L.A., 2025).

If I'd had a tracking system at 16, I would have noticed immediately that standing silently wasn't working. I would have adjusted my approach hours earlier, not after frustration finally kicked in.

The Power of Recovery

Built-in breaks between blocks matter as much as the selling itself. Use recovery periods for movement, short meditations, or standing outside for a few minutes. These micro-breaks reverse attention fatigue, sharpen mental focus, and help avoid burnout.

Many successful sellers add mini-reflections at lunch and late afternoon:

- What's working?

- What still feels slow?

- What needs attention tomorrow?

This keeps your actions aligned with the big picture.

Managing Distractions

To manage distractions, remove notifications when focus is required. Leave your phone in another room during prospecting blocks or use browser blockers to stay off social media. Prep desk setups the evening before—have leads ready, tools arranged, and your workspace clean. These small acts prime your brain for peak performance, much like athletes prepping gear before a big game.

Performance Reviews and Self-Renewal

Tracking personal performance turns vague ambition into direct actions. Use a daily scorecard to see your activity and outcomes, then review weekly for trends. For example, if your demo bookings sagged, try shifting them to your morning focus period the following week. Monthly reviews add another feedback loop. Chart progress on goals and habits: consistency builds over time and leads to better pipeline growth and win rates.

When energy dips or fatigue grows, long-term sales careers depend on self-renewal. This means using short breaks, fueling with healthy food, and sometimes saying no to low-impact meetings. Avoid overloading the calendar. Limit major selling efforts to your top two or three energy peaks, rather than scattering calls all day and burning out.

Celebrating small wins at the end of each day keeps motivation high, as does connecting with positive colleagues or mentors.

Consistency With Fundamentals

If you've built out your daily schedule and created time blocks for prospecting, there's one thing that makes it actually work: showing up and repeating those basics every single day. Consistency through repetition is where the magic really happens.

The Neuroscience of Repetition

Neuroscience tells us that repeating the same actions, like making calls or writing follow-up emails, actually rewires your brain to make those activities easier and more automatic over time. As you repeat these core sales actions, neural pathways get stronger. After a few weeks, something that once felt awkward is now second nature—like riding a bike or typing without looking at the keys.

The result is less mental friction and much faster reactions, precisely what's needed when you're under pressure or need to impress in a high-stakes interview (Chandrasekara, 2023).

The Power of Daily Basics

Top sales performers are masters of daily, repetitive basics. You'll hear them say things like, "I call fifty new prospects before noon, every workday. Rain or shine." That's not luck. That's discipline built on routine.

Another rep might review their call script out loud 10 times each morning and write down three new objections they expect to hear that day. The point isn't to go big once; it's to rack up those small wins again and again until they start to compound.

Making 50 calls each day for 30 days isn't just 1,500 calls. It's 30 opportunities to refine your intro, 1,500 chances to experiment with closing lines, and hundreds of moments to handle rejection and keep your confidence up.

Building Tactical Routines

Build these habits into your day with simple, tactical routines:

- **Warm up every morning:** Spend 10 minutes reciting your elevator pitch until it flows naturally

- **Do a call block:** Commit to dialing 25 leads before you even check your inbox

- **Keep track of objections:** Write down the tough ones, then practice responses during your lunch break

- **Send short recap emails:** Finish every client call with a two-sentence summary sent right away

- **Log and review:** Use a daily worksheet to mark how many contacts, referrals, and follow-ups you actually completed. At week's end, add up your totals and spot patterns

Daily Sales Practice Sheet

Here's a quick illustration of a daily sales practice sheet:

Date	Calls Made	Emails Sent	Meetings Booked	Objections Faced	Wins/Losses
Tues 10/3	52	17	2	7	1/1
Wed 10/4	48	21	3	5	2/0

It's easy to see progress or spot weak points at a glance.

Recovery Routines for Tough Days

Typically, challenges hit hard. No one escapes a run of bad days. Calls go to voicemail. Demos fizzle out. You might get hung up on five times in a row before your second coffee. These are the moments that test your commitment.

I experienced this standing outside that grocery store, watching person after person walk past me without even making eye contact. It stung. But instead of packing up and going home, I found a way to pivot. That resilience—even in its most unpolished, teenage form—made all the difference.

Elite sales reps don't shy away; they have recovery routines. If you're stung by a string of no's, here's a step-by-step bounce-back plan:

1. **Step away for 10 minutes:** Grab water, walk outside, or stretch out tension.

2. **Turn to your "Wins List":** Notes of past successes, even small ones.

3. **Say a quick mantra:** "Every no moves me closer to yes."

4. **Check your daily sheet:** Did you follow your script, or did you rush the pitch?

5. **Identify one thing to tweak:** Maybe use a different hook in your opener for your next block.

They might tell themselves, "Okay, today's not the day for new closes, but I can still master objections." Or run a visualization exercise: close your eyes, breathe deep, see yourself calmly handling a tough objection. Imagine winning the appointment. This approach rewires negative associations and brings back control.

How to Get a Sales Job

Landing your first sales role often means selling yourself with the same consistency, resilience, and strategic thinking it takes to succeed in sales. When you walk into the interview, treat it like your opening sales meeting. First, you present your differentiators. Then, you prove you care about their needs. Your words and your story must fit what your future manager actually wants.

Crafting Your Sales Interview Pitch

Start with the basics of a sales interview pitch: a sharp opening, proof of your value, concise delivery, and genuine enthusiasm. Good interviewers often start with "Tell me about yourself." Instead of reciting your resume, focus on value and results.

Here's a sample script:

"I'm someone who thrives when building trust with people and helping them solve problems. In my last job as a barista, I learned to listen to customers, remember details, and build a regular clientele. I also volunteered to upsell new menu items, and my shift had the highest product trial rate for our team."

Simple stories like this show the core sales qualities—resilience (adapting to feedback on the fly), consistency (showing up every day with a smile), and a mindset centered on helping (not pushing) people.

When I interview for sales positions now, I often share my perfume story. Not because I'm proud of lying—I'm not—but because it demonstrates quick thinking, emotional intelligence, and the ability to read a situation and adapt instantly. Those are the real skills that matter in sales.

Handling Common Questions

It helps to practice concise, punchy answers to common sales interview questions. For "Why should we hire you for sales with no direct experience?"

Try this:

"I've served people every day of my working life. From running front desk operations to handling complaints in retail, I learned how to make someone feel seen. I'm eager to bring that to a sales team, and I know I'll apply feedback quickly because I've always been coachable. For example, I turned around my customer service scores at my last job after only two weeks of coaching."

Sales managers want proof that you'll work at their pace, solve problems, and stay curious. These mini-scripts demonstrate resilience and coachability, and each ties your past wins to the employer's future wins.

The STAR Method for Behavioral Questions

Prepare for behavioral questions using the STAR method. Here's how that might play out:

Question: "Tell me about a time you worked toward a tough goal."

STAR method answer:

- **Situation:** "At my part-time delivery job, we needed to cut drop-off times."

- **Task:** "I was asked to help the team stay on schedule during our busiest week."

- **Action:** "I mapped out the route ahead of time and checked packages by ZIP code instead of street name."

- **Result:** "We finished forty minutes early, and my manager recognized me at the next all-hands meeting."

When you answer, focus on outcomes, not just the steps. The STAR method pushes you to name the results. Sales leaders always look for proof you're impact-driven.

Research the Company

Take time to research companies before each interview. Look up their products, company values, and press releases.

Make a quick list:

- top clients or industries they serve

- any recent product launches or news stories

- what their Glassdoor or LinkedIn reviewers highlight (work culture, management style)

Mention this research subtly. When they ask, "Why do you want to work here?" You can say: "I noticed your company just launched a mobile tool for property managers. I love tech that solves real problems, and I read that you prioritize customer satisfaction, which matches how I work best."

This shows preparation, curiosity, and a knack for connecting dots—skills that matter both in sales and job hunting.

Leveraging Transferable Skills

Not having "sales" in your job title doesn't mean you don't have relevant experience. Transferable skills often matter more. Make a list for yourself:

- **Relationship-building:** from food service, teaching, and coaching

- **Handling objections:** from customer service or tech support

- **Time management:** from balancing work and school

- **Communication:** from speaking, emailing, and writing quickly and persuasively

- **Fast learning and accepting feedback:** from learning from every challenge

For example:

"I didn't have sales targets in my last role, but my team set a goal to boost customer reviews. I suggested a follow-up checklist, and it improved our ratings by thirty percent over three months."

Even if you weren't in the official "sales" department, numbers and results carry weight.

Career Changers: Making the Connection

Let's say you're switching from a nursing background. In the interview, you might say this:

"Nurses need to build trust fast, communicate clearly under pressure, and overcome resistance to treatment, which aren't so different from sales conversations. I'm used to adapting and staying positive even with tough outcomes."

Employers care about attitude and effort as much as they do about work history. Saying, "I'm eager to learn, and I've always been quick to pick things up, whether it's new technology or customer processes," shows coachability. Offer to share a time when feedback made you stronger.

Stories from career changers make great proof points—like the teacher who brought energy and patience to her sales calls and closed her first deal in a month. Share past wins as evidence that you deliver and adapt quickly, and hiring managers will see you as a high-potential, low-risk hire (Deel, n.d.).

Wrapping It Up

From my awkward teenage self, standing silently with perfume bottles, to the structured, disciplined approach I developed over the years in sales, I've learned one fundamental truth: Sales is both an art and a science. The art is in reading people, connecting emotionally, and adapting in the moment. The science is in the systems, routines, and consistent habits that make success sustainable.

That day I sold 10 bottles of perfume wasn't the start of a great sales career; it was just a lucky break fueled by desperation and quick thinking. But the lessons from that experience—understanding emotional intelligence, having the courage to try even when it seems impossible, adapting instantly to changing situations—those became the foundation I built everything else on.

Now that you've seen how empathy, curiosity, resilience, and solid habits build the foundation for lasting sales success, it's time to put these ideas into action.

Remember, every call, every follow-up, and every learning moment adds up over time. So, take what you've learned here, start small, keep going, and watch as those habits become the powerful engine that drives your long-term success in sales and beyond.

Chapter 3:
Mastering the Cold Call

I don't know if I can do this, I remember thinking, staring at the phone during my first week in sales. *What if they just hang up?* That shaky feeling before a cold call is all too familiar: heart racing, palms sweaty, and a mind swirling with doubts.

But here's the thing: That fear isn't fixed. It can shift. What if instead of dread, you could pick up the phone with genuine confidence? The kind that comes from knowing exactly who you're talking to, what matters to them, and how to make those first few seconds count? Few things are as powerful as turning nervous energy into curiosity and connection. This chapter is all about making that shift happen.

Know Your Target Customer

Before you ever dial a number or compose your first cold-calling script, taking a little time to dig into who you're talking to can change everything. That flutter of dread that often comes with cold calls begins to fade when you realize you're not trying to win over a random stranger—you're reaching out to someone with clear interests, needs, and maybe even quirks you've just discovered.

I learned this the hard way. Early in my career, I'd simply dial down a list, hoping something would stick. The rejection was brutal because I had nothing to anchor the conversation to—no connection, no relevance, just a pitch thrown into the void. Everything changed when I started investing even five to ten minutes in research before each call. My thinking shifted from *Am I interrupting their day?* to *How can this call actually help them?* This simple shift quieted my pre-call nerves and armed me with real insights that sparked more natural, helpful conversations (Gibson, 2024).

The Research Process

It starts with setting aside the fear that looking up a person or company is intrusive. Think of it more like previewing a movie before buying a ticket—it just makes sense to know what you're getting into. First, go to the company's website. You'll often spot their mission, recent news, the person's job role, and sometimes even fun facts buried in team bios. On LinkedIn, you might see a recent work anniversary, a promotion, or posts that share what matters to this prospect. Glancing at press releases or even skimming a company's social media can reveal awards, partnerships, or big projects. You're not "spying" or digging up secrets; you're looking for the real hooks and touchpoints that can turn a stiff exchange into an easygoing, meaningful talk (Guler, 2025). You may find out they just expanded into a new market, or that your contact is speaking at an industry event soon. These small discoveries are golden.

Building Customer Personas

The real power here comes from building customer personas, not just keeping a list of companies and phone numbers. Creating a customer persona means giving each contact a little bit of story and color (Guler, 2025). Review what you've found: Who is the decision maker? What's their job title? How big is their team? Do they have control over budgets or processes that relate to your solution? Beyond dry details, pick up clues like favorite hobbies if those are public, or detect a style—maybe they use humor in their posts or comment on industry challenges. Grouping these little bits together turns a nameless contact into a person you can picture and relate to.

Putting Research to Work

When you put this knowledge to work, it pays off almost instantly. I remember one call where LinkedIn showed that someone had just been promoted. I opened with, "Congratulations on your new role, that's exciting!" The entire tone of the conversation shifted. She laughed, thanked me, and suddenly we were having an honest dialogue instead of a transactional pitch. Or if the company was featured in the news for a recent achievement, say, "I saw your team just won Best Workplace, that's awesome!" That kind of opener lowers defenses and shows you're genuinely interested. These cues aren't just about flattery—they let you ask thoughtful, relevant questions. Instead of "Do you have a budget for this?" you could say, "I noticed you're expanding; curious if you're tackling any new customer support challenges as you grow?" (Gibson, 2024).

Keeping these notes in a spreadsheet, notebook, or sticky note is enough. Don't overthink the system. Just track enough to jog your memory, and update after every chat.

Simple Exercise for Pre-Call Research

Taking action is easier when you have a small plan before picking up the phone. Give yourself a quick run-through by following these steps:

1. Pick one person or company from your outreach list. Make this manageable—just one at a time.

2. Set a five-minute timer and review their website, social media pages, and any news you can easily find. Don't get lost in the details; just look for what's new, notable, or shared frequently.

3. Write down two things: these could be interests, big company moves, or shared contacts (maybe you went to the same university or are in the same industry group).

4. Put together a short customer persona: list their job title, company size, recent business priorities, a couple of their interests, and anything that stands out about the way they communicate.

5. Come up with a question or compliment that connects to what you've found—maybe asking about a recent expansion or congratulating them on hitting a company milestone.

Preparing ahead gently replaces nervousness with genuine curiosity. When you have new details jotted down, you feel ready to have a back-and-forth, not just deliver a pitch. Pull out your notes right before the call so the conversation feels less like a cold transaction and more like a real, welcome introduction (Guler, 2025). Keep updating your persona as each call teaches you something new about the person or the company. Over time, you'll notice you're no longer winging it; you're reaching out with purpose and seeing better results with every call (Gibson, 2024).

Know Your Numbers

Being ready for a cold call does more than calm your nerves. Planning keeps you from dialing blindly—but it also means the numbers you start tracking actually mean something. Each time you pick up the phone or send an email, you're beginning a story of what works and what needs a little polish. Cold calling can feel like chaos, but tracking key metrics slices through all the guesswork. It's the difference between hoping for results and knowing whether you're actually getting closer to those first, confidence-boosting wins (Frost, 2023).

What to Track

There's no need for anything fancy at first. I started with a simple notebook—literally just tallying marks for each category. Grab a spreadsheet, a notebook, or an app on your phone and jot down the basics. Start with this:

- total calls made

- number of real conversations

- total voicemails left

- meaningful appointments set

- how many calls end up as genuine chances to close a deal

- average call length

Over the course of several days, these numbers show how much effort you're actually putting in and whether that effort is leading to even the smallest breakthroughs.

Learning From Your Data

Picture someone like Jamie, tracking every call for a week. Out of 50 calls, they have eight real conversations, leave 30 voicemails, and schedule one appointment. At first, it looks discouraging—*I'm failing 49 times for every "yes."* But seeing that most connections happened between noon and 1 p.m., Jamie tweaks their schedule. By week two, the same 50 calls turn into 15 conversations and three appointments just by shifting when the calls happen. That tiny change, discovered through tracking, suddenly feels like a superpower.

I experienced this myself. My early morning calls went straight to voicemail—every single one. But calls made right after lunch? People picked up. They'd just gotten back to their desks, had some energy from eating, and were more willing to engage. That one insight, discovered only because I was tracking my data, changed everything.

Tracking metrics isn't supposed to make you feel bad. The point is not to compare a new caller's numbers to someone who's been at it for years. Instead, the numbers form a ladder, showing steps toward real skill. Each improved call, longer conversation, or even each "better" rejection is progress.

Setting Realistic Expectations

Industry averages can help keep expectations sane (Frost, 2023). Most newcomers won't book a meeting with every handful of calls. For someone starting out, a call-to-close ratio could mean one booked meeting per 25 or even 30 calls, with a much smaller number actually closing. The numbers may feel harsh, but they're true for almost everyone. As confidence grows, those ratios improve—track closely, and you'll see changes over time.

Using Data to Improve

Measuring also lets you spot whether a tweak to your script or a new way of asking questions is working. If a slightly different greeting gets people talking for a minute instead of hanging up, write it down and test it all week. When you notice more people stay on the line after using a new fact you researched about their company, add that info to your playbook. Even watching how long your average call lasts can be an early sign that you're moving from awkward, rushed pitches to real human conversations.

Goal-setting goes hand in hand with tracking. It's not about making giant leaps right away. Try setting a goal like having just one real conversation every day this week, then bumping up total daily calls by 10%. If you log those attempts and see even small gains, that's the fuel for future confidence. Significant progress hides in routine improvement (Georgeson, 2024).

Celebrate the inches. Maybe you didn't get a "yes" today, but you learned when people answer, which questions make them pause, and how to keep someone on the line longer than ever before. All of that is visible through your record-keeping. Over time, your personalized stats will be proof—a nudge that you're growing. When you spot that your calls per day are trending up, or that even one more person is saying yes to an appointment, you're seeing confidence take root in your actions (Frost, 2023).

The First Few Seconds

Cold calling isn't a game where every throw lands a perfect score. The reality is that most calls will end without a win, and some will end after just a few words. While call tracking and hard numbers help you see the big picture, the true test happens in that awkward space when someone answers the phone and you have just a sliver of time to catch their attention. What you do in those first seconds decides if you'll hear a click or a curious question.

Avoiding Common Traps

The most common trap is starting with old, stiff phrases that scream "sales call." Think of "Hi, how are you today?" or "Can I take a minute of your time?" These lines make recipients put up a guard or even speed-dial the hang-up button. Instead, use openers that feel real and give people a reason to stay. A bold, honest opener is more engaging than a safe, forgettable one.

Weak Approach

"Hi, this is Mike with Global Tech Solutions. How are you today?"

[Pause. Recipient sighs.] "I'm good."

"I'm just calling to see if you might be interested in our IT services?"

[Click.]

Strong Approach

"Hi, this is Mike from Global Tech. I saw your company just opened a new office downtown—congrats. I'm calling with a quick idea about saving your team time with new scheduling tools. Is this a good time?"

[Pause. Recipient listens, maybe asks a question.]

This variation leads with something specific to the recipient and gives context. The opener is clear, upbeat, and doesn't feel scripted (Intelemark, 2025).

Effective Opening Strategies

You can sharpen your opener by strongly avoiding the tension-killing question, "Is now a bad time?" Instead, try asking for quick help, which feels less pushy. For example: "Hey [Name], I was hoping you could help me out really quick." This opener is humble and lowers resistance because people often want to help when asked.

Another option is a confident acknowledgment: "I know you get plenty of these calls. I promise to be brief and hopefully helpful—do you have a moment?" These styles display self-awareness and respect (*Avoiding Hang-Ups*, 2025).

Sharp openers often pose a question—either direct or implied. A line like "I noticed ABC Company just launched a new product—can you spare a minute to hear how others are handling early feedback?" connects to something current, shows the caller did homework, and addresses a real business need without drowning the recipient in details. When you show you've prepared for the call, you build trust faster (Intelemark, 2025).

Handling Early Resistance

Skillful cold callers also know what to do when resistance pops up right at the start. Imagine the answer is a flat "I'm not interested." Instead of folding, you can calmly say, "No problem, may I ask what you're focusing on right now?" Or, "That makes sense. Out of curiosity, how are you handling [topic] these days?" These responses lower tension and may spark a short, meaningful exchange without pressure.

Building on these techniques, use openers that get prospects to say yes early in the call. Simple confirmations like "Am I speaking with Michael? Are you still leading the sales team?" set up a chain of agreement. This makes it harder for people to hang up, and gets them used to saying yes instead of no (*Avoiding Hang-Ups*, 2025).

Your Voice Is Your Power

When the first few seconds of your cold call come alive with the right energy, interest usually follows. A winning opening line grabs a person's attention, but it's the energy you wrap around each word—the very sound of your voice—that unlocks the real conversation.

Here's something most people don't realize: On the phone, you lose about 40% of your natural tone, emotion, and energy (Russell, 2023). Think about that. Nearly half of what makes you engaging in person simply doesn't translate through the receiver. The top sales reps I've worked with compensate for this by being louder, clearer, and more authoritative than they'd ever be face-to-face. It's not about yelling or being rude; it's about projecting confidence in a way that replaces all the body language you'd generally use in person.

Your voice is literally all you have on a cold call. Voice projection equals authority, and authority builds trust. When you speak with a strong, clear phone tone, you control the conversation. People listen. They stay engaged. They believe what you're saying because the way you say it signals competence and certainty.

Voices That Spark Connection

I learned this lesson early on. Imagine this scene: Two callers work down the same list. One reads the script almost mechanically. Their pitch never moves, their words sound flat, and each "hello" blends into the next. The other—me, on a good day—decides to add a smile. Though no one sees it, it colors the tone. I brighten my greeting, almost singing the first few syllables. Suddenly, the response changes. Instead of silence or a polite "not interested," prospects become curious. They pause, listen, and join the dialogue. That cheerful injection of personality signals, without a word, "I care if you listen." The enthusiasm is contagious because it expresses self-assurance and genuine interest.

Energy in your voice sends a silent message: "This call matters—to me, and maybe to you too." Prospects pick up on it right away, even through static or digital delays. A monotone, by contrast, signals boredom or nervousness. But a "smile-in-your-voice" flips the script. Listeners find themselves automatically trusting voices that sound upbeat, steady, and friendly.

Picture Sofia. Her early cold calls sounded robotic, right down to the last syllable. Each pitch was word-perfect but lifeless. One day, a mentor suggested, "Try pretending you're calling a good friend." Sofia hesitated, then pictured her sister's face, added warmth to her greeting, paused between lines, and let her inflection rise and fall. The prospect chuckled and answered, "You sound like you actually want to talk." Conversation blossomed.

Balancing Passion and Professionalism

Expressing excitement helps, but too much can overwhelm. Sounding overly eager or a little frantic can create suspicion or pushback. Finding the middle ground is about subtle but powerful shifts:

- Lower your pitch slightly to make your voice sound calmer and more composed.

- Allow a pause after key phrases to create emphasis and draw in listeners.

- Slow your speech just a bit to give words time to land and show confidence.

Lynette, a salesperson I trained with, noticed that speaking too fast left her breathless and prospects confused. She tried pausing for two heartbeats after her introduction. The call slowed down, but her words sounded steadier. The person on the other end asked a follow-up instead of cutting her off.

Confidence is something listeners can hear—and you can develop it. Speaking with intention, switching up tempo and inflection, and acting as if you're chatting with someone you know well sends the message that you belong in the conversation. Remember: Your voice replaces everything—your handshake, your posture, your eye contact. Make it count.

Exercise: Sounding the Part

Try building awareness and vocal control with this simple exercise:

1. Choose a short cold call script.

2. Record yourself reading it in your usual work voice.

3. Record again, this time smiling, adding energy, and giving yourself permission to exaggerate, as if you are genuinely excited.

4. Listen to both recordings. Notice your mood, energy, and sense of confidence as you playback each version.

5. Ask yourself which one you would trust and want to talk to if you were the prospect.

6. Repeat with different scripts and emotions to find your "sweet spot" of authenticity and enthusiasm.

Every word you say, and every bit of energy behind it, shows the kind of confidence you want to feel—even if you have to "fake it" sometimes at first.

Body Language Over the Phone

The way a person carries themselves and shapes their face—whether or not anyone on the other end can see—matters just as much as vocal tone when it comes to cold calling. Mindset leaks through the line, turning a flat or hesitant approach into a solid, positive first impression, even if the listener never sees a face or posture.

Stand vs. Sit

The debate over standing versus sitting during a cold call comes up in every advice book and sales meeting, but the difference is dramatic. I used to sit at my desk, slouched back with rounded shoulders, maybe letting my chin tuck in, eyes drifting to my computer screen. When I'd call someone in that position, my words came out muffled, tentative, swallowed at the ends of sentences. Breath felt restrained, the jaw moved less, and my voice's power shrank.

Then one day, frustrated with a string of terrible calls, I stood up. I adjusted my feet so I was balanced, let my shoulders fall back, and breathed deeply. I tried my pitch again, and the difference was instant. Standing pushed my voice into a higher-energy place. I could literally hear myself sounding stronger, more certain, more like someone worth listening to. Listeners actually sense this shift in a way that goes further than words; there's more brightness, steadiness, and certainty. When nerves hit, standing tall can even counteract fidgeting or mumbling, letting the natural "executive" presence slip into the call.

The Power of Smiling

Beyond posture, the invisible superpower for phone calls is smiling. It's common advice, but let me get real: The quality of a smile can change a greeting from bland to magnetic. Say, "Good afternoon, this is Jamie calling from..." with a tight mouth and unmoved cheeks. It sounds flat, formal, and maybe a bit cold. Try the same line while letting a genuine, relaxed smile break out. Suddenly, the tone warms, vowels stretch, and listeners hear what researchers call "vocal sunshine," the inaudible but deeply felt vibe of someone cheerful, approachable, and calm. Smiling even changes how you pace yourself; the brain reads body cues for calmness and comfort, sending a feedback loop that can actually lower nerves and help you speak with better rhythm (Team AASC, 2025).

Practical Drill

For cold callers seeking real progress, here's a step-by-step, try-this-at-home exercise designed to build awareness and control over these hidden tools:

1. Take a moment to stand up straight or, if sitting, to bring your body into a strong, alert position. Shoulders back, feet planted, spine long.

2. Put on a genuine smile—not the forced kind, but one you could wear in a light conversation with a friend. Tune in to how even a private smile feels.

3. Imagine dialing a prospect. Recite your cold-call pitch or talking points as naturally as possible.

4. Record yourself using your phone or computer. No re-dos or edits—just the real, raw pitch.

5. Play it back, listening for tone (Does your voice ring out with positivity?), clarity (Can you hear each word cleanly?), and pacing (Any signs of rushing from nerves or slowing from uncertainty?).

6. Give yourself a mini-review—pick just one thing to adjust, like posture, bigger smile, or speed. Try the call again, record, and compare.

7. Jot down which subtle tweaks make you sound better and why you think they worked.

No need to chase perfection. Awkwardness is proof you're growing. Maybe the first version sounds tight or hurried; often, the next take, with just a smile or a posture fix, comes out brighter and easier. Each round builds muscle memory, lending confidence and fluency for when real calls begin.

Even though listeners can't see you, your physiology shapes every sound you make. A poised body frees the breath and natural pace. A relaxed, alert face releases tension, making you sound warmer and kinder. In turn, all this care behind the scenes pours out in a more magnetic voice, changing outcomes. With practice, these tricks become automatic, letting you show up for each cold call as the most persuasive, steady version of yourself—one whose confidence is unmistakable and contagious (Asian Institute of Management, 2025).

Wrapping It Up

Now that you've learned how to turn fear into confidence by really knowing your customer, tracking your progress, mastering the first few seconds, and using your voice and body to connect, you're ready to take cold calling from something scary to something powerful. Each call becomes less about hoping for a win and more about building authentic conversations, step by step.

I won't lie: Cold calling never becomes easy. There are still days when I pick up the phone and feel that flutter of nerves. But the difference now is that I have tools, systems, and proven techniques that work. I know my research gives me relevance. I know my numbers show me progress. I know my voice, when I use it right, carries authority and warmth that cuts through the phone line's limitations.

With every bit of research, every number tracked, and every smile through the phone, you're shaping a new kind of confidence—one that grows with practice and shows up in your tone, your words, and the energy you bring. So, go ahead, pick up that phone with purpose, because now you have the tools to make each call count and move closer to the success you're aiming for.

Chapter 4:
How to Handle Objections

Have you ever felt stuck when someone says no or pushes back on an idea? Maybe it's a friend who dodges plans, a coworker who resists a new process, or a client who shoots down your pitch before you can explain. What if handling those objections didn't have to feel tense or awkward? What if, instead of hearing "no" as a roadblock, you could see it as the start of a real conversation—one where listening carefully and shifting your tone could open doors instead of shutting them?

This chapter explores how small changes in timing, voice, and attitude can transform resistance into connection, making objections feel less like battles and more like chances to build trust. If you've ever wondered how to keep conversations flowing even when faced with doubt or hesitation, you're about to discover some surprisingly simple tools to make that happen.

Learning to Collect Money: The Ultimate Leadership Lesson

Before I dive into objection-handling techniques, let me tell you about the experience that taught me more about handling resistance than any sales training ever could.

When I was 17, my sales manager taught me how to collect unpaid invoices. Watching him chase down $20,000, $30,000, even $40,000 payments with absolute confidence was like studying a master at work. Some customers lied. Some avoided calls. Some flat-out refused to pay.

That's when I learned my first hard truth: Buyers lie. Not to hurt you—but to protect their advantage.

This wasn't cynical; it was practical. Most customers don't care about your paycheck. They care about themselves: their budget, their needs, their timing. Once I understood this, I stopped taking objections personally and started seeing them for what they really were: protective mechanisms, not personal attacks.

For three months as a 17-year-old salesman, I hardly had any sales under my belt. Then, something clicked. A customer canceled an order on me. I was devastated. But my manager grabbed the phone, offered the customer a 40% discount, and saved the sale instantly.

Watching that opened my eyes: You can save almost any deal if you're willing to work with the customer. It was the first time I saw negotiation as a tool—not a weakness. That moment changed everything about how I approached objections.

I began studying reactions, tone changes, objections, excuses, and patterns. I'd watch how customers' faces shifted when they were uncomfortable versus when they were genuinely interested but cautious. I noticed that the objection someone led with was rarely the real obstacle—it was just the safest thing to say first. Over time, I learned to wait for the second or third concern, the one that came out quieter, almost apologetically. That was usually the truth.

Slowly, I built my customer base—50, 60, then 70+ customers—and eventually discovered a repeat-business strategy that gave me 80% retention, a system I still use today.

Timing of Rebuttals

A tense moment at the dinner table, a challenging client call, a coworker pushing back on a deadline—objection handling isn't just for sales professionals. Everyone, at some point, finds themselves on either side of resistance. It can feel awkward, or even intimidating, to face someone who says "No," "Not now," or "I'm not sure." When tension rises, reading the room and adjusting your timing and your voice can be the secret ingredient that changes everything.

The Power of Pauses

Imagine yourself negotiating a budget with a manager who frowns and folds their arms. You launch into your well-prepared pitch, but the lack of response makes your heart thud. Many people's instinct is to fill the silence, to rush through more reasons or repeat their main point. Yet, sitting with a pause, while holding a steady, calm energy, often works better. Silence can coax out real objections that might stay buried if you come across as pushy or nervous (*Difficult Conversations*, 2023).

I learned this while watching my manager collect those unpaid invoices. He never rushed. When a customer made an excuse, he'd go quiet— just for a moment—and let the silence do the work. More often than not, the customer would fill that space with the real reason they hadn't paid.

The psychology behind this is fascinating. When you pause after someone voices an objection, you create a vacuum that humans are naturally compelled to fill. In that moment of silence, the other person often realizes their initial objection sounds hollow or incomplete, even to themselves. They'll frequently add clarifying details, reveal deeper concerns, or soften their stance without you saying a word.

For example, a salesperson notices a client growing quiet after a pricing discussion. Instead of jumping in, she smiles gently and waits. The client eventually sighs, "I'm worried about ongoing support. Will your team be there?" Only after the pause does the true concern surface, revealing a new opportunity to address it together.

Using pauses takes conscious effort, especially when you want to convince someone. This skill doesn't just mean saying nothing; it means holding space with purpose. Your facial expression and posture, just like your voice, complete the picture. Raising your eyebrows slightly or giving a reassuring nod shows you're listening. This is woven into the LAER method—listen, acknowledge, explore, respond— which encourages you to fully listen and explore before moving to solutions (Wolf, 2025).

The timing of your pause matters too. A half-second hesitation won't do much. You need to be comfortable with three to five seconds of silence, which feels like an eternity when you're anxious to respond. Count slowly in your head if you need to. Watch the other person's eyes, their hands, the way they shift their weight.

Gentle Persistence

Sometimes, gentle persistence makes all the difference. When a prospect says, "I'm not sure if it'll work for us right now," a good response would be, "What would make the timing right for you? Is there something specific holding you back?" This approach recognizes the objection without turning up the pressure, keeping the conversation open and honest.

Remember my manager saving that canceled order with a 40% discount? That wasn't desperation; it was strategic persistence. He understood that a saved deal at a lower margin beats a lost deal every time and that customers often need to feel they've won something to move forward.

Gentle persistence isn't about badgering or wearing someone down through repetition. It's about maintaining your presence in the conversation without dominating it. Think of it like holding a door open: You're not pushing anyone through, but you're making it clear the option remains available.

The Role of Tone

Tone shapes the outcome just as much as timing. Too often, people respond to resistance with sharp comebacks or a rushed, clipped voice, which triggers defensiveness and closes off possibilities. Contrast that with someone lowering their voice, slowing down, and adding a note of empathy. A calm, warm sound signals respect and invites the other person to lower their guard (*Difficult Conversations*, 2023).

Think about how you feel when someone raises their voice or speaks faster when you express doubt: Your shoulders tighten, your jaw sets, and you prepare to defend your position even more strongly. Now, imagine the opposite: Someone responds to your concern by speaking more softly, more slowly, with genuine warmth in their voice. Your body relaxes. Your mind opens.

Disagreement does not have to feel like a scolding; it can sound like curiosity. For example, saying, "I hear your concern about needing more flexibility. Would you like to talk through a few ways we could support that?" conveys a willingness to adapt, turning the objection into a shared puzzle to solve.

Your vocal tone communicates intention faster than your words. Before your brain processes what someone is saying, it's already categorized how they're saying it—friendly or hostile, confident or desperate, genuine or manipulative. This happens in milliseconds and colors everything that follows.

Practice Exercise

Practice pausing during a safe conversation. When a friend or family member expresses doubt or disagreement, resist the urge to respond right away.

1. Count to three in your mind while keeping eye contact.

2. Watch their body language and tone.

3. Notice if they fill the silence, relax, or share more information.

4. Test using a softer tone with your next reply: lower your volume slightly, slow down, and say, "That's a good point. Tell me more about what worries you."

5. Reflect after each experiment: Did the mood shift? Did the other person open up?

After trying the exercise, you'll see how even minor tweaks to your timing and delivery can melt tension or prevent a conversation from shutting down completely.

Diminishing the Objection

A raised voice or careful pause only tells part of the story. Real connection grows from what you do when you sense resistance in the room. The first impulse after hearing a sharp "That'll never work here" may be to stack up arguments to prove otherwise. Yet, there's a gentler way to sidestep a standoff: treating objections not as barriers, but as curious invitations.

Validation and Redirection

Instead of tightening up when met with, "This system doesn't work for me," you might take a measured breath and say, "I can see that's frustrating. What would help it feel a bit better?" This approach, centering on validation, helps release the emotional charge in moments of pushback. When you ask a question that looks past the stated problem, you invite fresh thinking and plant hope, even if answers aren't immediate.

At the root of this approach is a concept supported by research: Validation eases the fear of being judged, even when someone disagrees or resists (Hoek et al., 2025). When a person feels understood in the moment—even when they are upset or combative—a layer of tension peels away. It doesn't mean agreeing with the objection; it means showing that its existence, and the feeling underneath, matter enough to consider before you push for change.

Validation is powerful because it separates the person from their objection. When you validate someone's concern, you're essentially saying, "You're reasonable for thinking this way, given your experience and perspective." This removes the need for them to defend their position because you're not attacking it.

A sequence that works well: First notice and acknowledge the concern ("That's a tough spot"), then gently direct attention toward the person's ideas about improvement ("If this could work a little better, what would need to shift?"). The redirect is crucial. Without it, validation alone can reinforce the objection, making it feel more legitimate and permanent.

The Power of Empathy

Empathic communication during tense moments, especially when paired with curiosity, paves the way to resolution. Studies show that even brief moments of genuine interest can improve relationships and outcomes (*Training Magazine*, n.d.). In tense exchanges, this same structure can be repurposed: acknowledge, validate, and invite input. For example, if someone objects, "Our team never has enough time," a rapport-building reply could sound like, "Time pressure is real. What could make this feel less rushed for you?"

Empathy doesn't mean agreement. You can understand why someone feels a certain way without endorsing their conclusion. This distinction is vital. True empathy sits in the middle. It acknowledges the other person's emotional reality while keeping the conversation open to new possibilities.

When I was collecting those invoices, empathy was my most valuable tool. I'd hear "Business is terrible, I can't possibly pay right now," and instead of arguing about their business performance, I'd say, "Cash flow crunches are brutal—I've been there. What's a realistic amount you could put toward this today?" This approach acknowledged their struggle without accepting that non-payment was the only option.

Building Your Response Arsenal

Try it for yourself. Write a list of three objections you hear in your daily work—maybe from colleagues, clients, or family. Next to each, craft a response that acknowledges the feeling and redirects toward a brighter possibility.

Examples:

- "That's a fair concern. What would need to change for this to work?"

- "I get why this feels too much. Tell me what would make it manageable."

- "It's true, we've hit some snags before. In a perfect world, how does this go smoothly?"

Read the objection, then practice your response in the mirror or with a friend. Focus on softening your tone, and listen to whether you sound more hopeful when you ask these new questions.

Having these responses prepared prevents you from fumbling when objections arise. Build your arsenal by category. Group similar objections together—price objections, timing objections, competitor objections, internal resistance objections. For each category, develop three to five go-to responses that feel natural when you say them.

Strategic Use of Humor

Sometimes, a moment of humor slides open a window where tension once pressed in hard. When objections start to stack up—"You always suggest wild ideas!"—a playful, "I do have a talent for thinking outside the box, don't I?" can invite a smile and signal that you're open to meeting resistance without shutting down.

This isn't about making light of real pain or dismissing strong feelings. Humor lands best when everyone feels heard and there's room for gentle, mutual ribbing. There are times, though, when an empathic response works better than a laugh. Saying, "It makes total sense why you'd hesitate," or "That would throw anyone for a loop," soothes defensiveness. People open up when they sense the person in front of them is genuinely leaning in to understand (*Training Magazine*, n.d.).

Don't Repeat Negatives

Negative words have a stubborn way of sticking around. Bring them up over and over in conversations, and they get even stronger. That's why avoiding the repetition of objections during talks matters so much. It's not just about what's said once, but about what your brain hangs onto when you or someone else repeats a point, especially a negative one.

Research on memory shows that negative content gets encoded more deeply and lasts longer than neutral or even happy memories. Every time a negative thought or objection is mentioned, it gets highlighted again in the mind, making it feel more vivid and true (Vaish et al., 2008).

I discovered this during my invoice collection days. When a customer said, "I can't pay because business is slow," my instinct was to repeat it back: "So, business is slow, and you can't pay?" Bad move. That just reinforced their excuse in both our minds. Instead, I learned to redirect: "What would help us find a way to get this resolved this month?"

Real-World Impact

You can see this play out at work. Maybe someone says, "Customers always complain about our response time." The easy instinct is to nod and say, "Yes, people are always complaining." On the surface, this seems empathetic. Instead, it cements the complaint as a permanent reality. It becomes part of the team's shared memory. Over time, this statement can become a self-fulfilling prophecy, because everyone expects more complaints, notices them more, and ignores any opposite evidence.

Think about how company cultures develop around repeated negative narratives. "We're always behind schedule" becomes a badge of identity rather than a problem to solve. "Leadership never listens" turns into an accepted truth that nobody questions. These narratives persist because people keep repeating them, strengthening the neural pathways associated with those beliefs each time they're voiced.

Reframing Instead of Repeating

What can you do instead? The answer is to reframe, not repeat. Instead of saying, "So, the issue is that our projects always fall behind?" try:

"Sounds like we want to find ways to finish projects more smoothly next time." Redirect the message, focusing forward. Replace "never," "always," or "nobody" with practical, active language.

Practical Reframing Examples

Workplace Disagreement

- **Before:** "We're never going to hit this deadline."

- **After:** "Let's explore steps we can take to move the deadline, or see which parts are most urgent right now."

Customer Service

- **Before:** "You're saying this product never works like it should?"

- **After:** "I want to understand what the product is not doing for you. Let's find a fix that gets you what you need."

Personal Discussion

- **Before:** "So, you don't trust me?"

- **After:** "What would help you feel more comfortable with this?"

Every time you pick the second phrase, you shift attention away from what cannot be done and toward what can. Use phrases that open doors rather than reinforce the same cycles. Responses like "What options do we have?" or "What would a win look like here?" move conversations forward without brushing aside the emotions behind objections (Vaish et al., 2008).

Notice how the reframed versions often include questions. This is deliberate. Questions engage the problem-solving part of someone's brain rather than the defensive, reactive part. When you ask, "What would help?" you're inviting collaboration.

Stop Listening to Automatic Objections

When someone hears "no" or gets pushback, the first reaction is often to tense up or retreat. That discomfort comes from thinking the objection is a threat to the sale, the relationship, or your own confidence. It's completely normal. Everyone's had that flush of anxiety when a customer raises a worry or flat out rejects an idea.

What makes a difference is whether you let that reaction call the shots.

Understanding Automatic Objections

Try thinking of "no" as an opening, not a closed door. People offer objections for all kinds of reasons—sometimes out of habit, because they've been trained to protect themselves, or just because it's easier to say no than to dig deeper. Sometimes, those objections have nothing to do with you or your offer.

Remember: Buyers lie to protect their advantage. This isn't malicious; it's human nature. Understanding this freed me from taking every "no" at face value. Instead, I started asking: *What's the real concern underneath this automatic response?*

Most objections function as social scripts—learned responses that people deploy without much thought because they've worked before. "I need to think about it" isn't usually about needing time to think. It's a socially acceptable way to end a conversation when someone feels pressured or uncertain. "It's too expensive" often means "I don't see enough value yet" or "I haven't prioritized this in my budget."

Spotting Habitual Objections

Spotting a habitual objection takes practice. Next time you're in a sales situation, listen carefully to what the other person is saying. If their objection comes out quickly, without much detail or thought, it's probably automatic. These might sound like:

- "That's too expensive."

- "I need to think about it."

- "We already have a supplier."

Don't rush to fix these right away. Take a breath and ask a gentle follow-up, like "Can you tell me more about what you were expecting?" or "What would make this feel like a better fit for you?" When you meet these objections with curiosity instead of resistance, nine times out of ten you'll uncover what's really driving them.

The test for whether an objection is automatic is simple: Does it invite conversation or shut it down? Real objections are specific. They contain details about the person's situation, concerns about particular features, or references to past experiences. Automatic objections are generic. They could apply to any product, any service, any conversation. When you hear generic, that's your signal to dig deeper.

Preemptive Objection Handling

Preemptive objection handling is another skill that saves time and builds credibility. This means addressing potential concerns before your customer even raises them. For example, a savvy advisor might say, "We know some people expect longer wait times, so we offer courtesy transportation. Most of our customers love this convenience," or "Some clients have had concerns about value, which is why we break down every charge on your invoice." Doing this lets you control the narrative and sets your customer at ease, reducing their urge to object automatically.

When you voice an objection before the customer does, you accomplish several things simultaneously. First, you demonstrate that you understand their world and the concerns people in their position typically have. Second, you get to frame the objection and its resolution on your terms. Third, you show confidence. People who are hiding something don't bring up potential problems.

Role Playing for Mastery

Spotting patterns in the objections you hear is only the start. Real improvement comes when you take those patterns and bring them to life so you can practice handling the uncomfortable moments, not just analyze them.

My manager was the first person to push me into role-playing exercises. At first, I thought it was silly—pretending to have sales conversations seemed pointless. But he insisted: "Great mentors challenge you, not comfort you." He was right. Those practice sessions built the muscle memory I needed when real money was on the line.

Testing Different Approaches

Grab a friend—maybe a coworker or someone who knows how to keep a straight face when you pitch—and ask them to be a "tough customer." Give them objections you've been facing: "I really don't have the budget," or "I want to talk with my partner first."

On your first run, your friend says, "Honestly, I'm happy with my current supplier." You answer off the top of your head. They might push back harder. This is the cue to test different responses:

- **Softer approach:** "I totally get that. You need reliability. If you ever look for more flexible options, I can show you some ways people like you have saved money."

- **Empathy-heavy angle:** "Sounds like you've had a good experience, and you don't want to change what's working. May

I ask, What would make you consider something new, just in case your needs change later?"

After each exchange, pause and talk together. Did the response feel natural or too forced? Did your tone match your intention? This is exactly what negotiation training emphasizes—separating people from problems, using empathy, showing you've heard them, and reframing to move the conversation forward (Soni, 2025).

The beauty of role-playing is that it creates a safe space for failure. You can test responses that might be too risky to try with real customers. You can experiment with tone, pacing, and wording until you find what works.

Building Your Rebuttal Library

To make this practice stick, you need a living library of rebuttals—a place where you stash the best responses you've discovered. Picture a note on your phone divided by objection type. Under "Let me think about it," jot down tested replies:

- "Absolutely, take your time. Do you want any more info while you're considering?"

- "Of course. Would next Tuesday work for a check-in so you've got a chance to look things over?"

Make notes on which answer felt like you, which felt awkward, and which got a positive response. Your library might also include favorite stories, good analogies, or open-ended questions that keep the conversation alive.

This is the system that helped me build 80% retention with my customer base. Every objection I encountered became a lesson, every response I tested became data, and over time, I developed an instinct for what works.

Quick Practice Exercise

To get started right now:

1. Call up a peer and trade places: one person is the customer, the other is you.

2. The "customer" picks from a list of real objections you've faced—or invents a new one.

3. The "rep" answers with two or three approaches they've been wanting to work on.

4. After each run-through, the customer rates which felt most natural and convincing.

5. Switch parts and repeat.

After 15 minutes, you'll have both built confidence and harvested new lines for your rebuttal library. Just as arguing to learn sharpens reasoning, iterating these responses out loud helps you master the social dynamics of real negotiation.

Wrapping It Up

Now that you've learned how to turn resistance into rapport by using smart timing, a calm tone, and thoughtful responses, you're ready to take these skills out into the real world. Remember, objections aren't roadblocks; they're openings for connection if you listen closely, pause just right, and choose your words carefully.

The lessons I learned chasing unpaid invoices at 17—that buyers protect their interests, that negotiation is a tool not a weakness, that great mentors push you—these have shaped every interaction I've had since. With practice and maybe some fun role-playing with friends, handling pushback can become second nature instead of stressful.

Keep building your personal library of go-to replies and fresh questions so you always have something ready to ease tension and keep conversations moving forward. As you try these approaches in your daily life—whether at work, with family, or in tough meetings—you'll find it easier to steer toward understanding and possibilities, not just getting stuck on no.

The transformation from seeing objections as threats to seeing them as opportunities doesn't happen overnight. It requires consistent practice, honest reflection, and a willingness to learn from both successes and failures. But the payoff is enormous. When you master objection handling, you gain confidence in every conversation. You stop dreading pushback and start welcoming it as a chance to understand what people really need.

Start today. Pick one technique from this chapter—maybe it's the power of pauses, maybe it's reframing instead of repeating negatives, maybe it's building your rebuttal library. Practice it in a low-stakes conversation. Pay attention to what changes. Then add another technique, and another. Before long, you'll find yourself navigating objections smoothly and naturally, turning what once felt like confrontation into genuine connection.

Chapter 5:
Understanding the Close

Most people think closing a sale is just about getting someone to sign on the dotted line or swipe their card. But here's the thing: Closing isn't really about the paperwork at all. It's about that moment when both sides—buyer and seller—take a leap of trust, hope, and yes, sometimes a bit of fear.

That split second where a decision moves from "thinking about it" to "doing it" is packed with more emotion and subtle signals than most people realize. Understanding what's really happening in those final moments can change everything—not just how deals get made, but how people feel about saying yes.

The Day I Accidentally Summoned a Ghost Dog

I learned this lesson in the most unexpected way when I was about 16 and a half, selling high-end industrial vacuums door to door. These weren't your average discount store specials—no, these were premium, NASA-level suction machines priced at $2,500. The kind of vacuum that could probably pull the dents out of your car if you tried hard enough.

The company told me something very motivating: Sell it for anything over $1,750 and you get a commission. At 16 years old, the math was simple. Sell vacuum, get money, become rich.

The appointment setter lined up three houses for me that day. The first two were no-sales. By the time I got to the third house, I was praying someone would at least offer me a glass of water.

An older woman in her 70s opened the door. Sweet lady. The kind of grandma who probably makes cookies that heal childhood trauma. As part of my professional sales technique, I politely asked if I could take off my tie and roll up my sleeves before starting the demonstration. She agreed, and the show began.

I kicked off my performance by dropping sand into the vacuum canister, then flipped the vacuum upside-down. No sand fell out. Not a grain. Then, I dramatically dropped two steel balls into the sand, turned the vacuum upside down again, and they stuck like they'd signed a lease in there. She was impressed, but not sold.

Then, she asked the dreaded question: "So... how much is it?"

I delivered the line: "It's $2,500."

Her soul temporarily left her body. "That's... very expensive."

I knew I needed to bring out the big guns—the clear lid demonstration. This is where you vacuum a spot on the carpet and show the customer the dirt they didn't know existed. I asked where a good place to vacuum would be. She said she'd already vacuumed that day, but to try over by the fireplace.

I turned on the vacuum. Dirt started showing up in the clear lid—great! Then, more dirt. Then suddenly, a giant puff of black pet hair shot up. Then another. And another. It looked like I was vacuuming the ghost of a long-haired Rottweiler.

I turned to her and asked, "Ma'am... do you have a dog?"

She stared at the vacuum, eyes wide, and suddenly burst into tears. I froze. What did I do?

Between sobs, she said, "That's... that's my dog's hair. That's where he used to lie... He's been gone for ten years!"

Ten years. This vacuum wasn't just strong—it resurrected memories. She wasn't just emotional; she was reliving a decade-old bond with her late pet, courtesy of my vacuum's industrial-grade extraction system.

She wiped her eyes and asked, "How much did you say the vacuum was?"

I hesitated. "$2,500..."

"I'll take it."

She wrote me a check on the spot. The vacuum didn't just clean her carpet—it cleaned her soul.

That day taught me one of the most significant truths in sales: People buy on emotion. Happy, sad, shocked, nostalgic—doesn't matter. Emotion sells. I didn't just sell a vacuum. I sold peace of mind, closure, and the removal of a decade-old dog imprint.

Defining the Close

When people talk about "the close" in sales, most imagine a moment where someone signs on the dotted line, swipes a card, or shakes hands to seal the deal. But a close is more than a transaction or a formal agreement. It's the moment when both the seller and the buyer make a real human leap that goes way beyond paperwork.

On one side, you have someone handing over money or commitment. On the other, you have a person taking responsibility and making a promise. Both sides feel a surge of emotion—a mix of nerves, hope, and sometimes straight-up fear. The close is the point where trust becomes action and where doubts have to give way, even if only for a moment.

The Buyer's Journey to Yes

There's a real intensity in the moments leading up to a close. Think about the last time you almost bought something expensive or committed to a new membership or contract. Maybe you were test-driving a car for the third time, running your hand over the steering wheel, or you were at a gym, glancing at the contract and wondering about your monthly budget. Your mind probably raced with questions: *Am I getting a good deal? Am I sure about this? Will I regret this tomorrow?*

Buyers usually pass through a few common stages as they inch closer to a yes. They start with curiosity and a bit of excitement—maybe even hope. They're imagining how their life could look with this new thing. Then, doubts slip in: *Is this the right fit? What if I run into problems?* As the seller answers questions and clears up worries, the buyer weighs the value and risk in their head.

Time pressure can push them to make a quick call, especially if there's a limited-time offer or stock is running out. This urgency can make emotions boil up, sometimes leading to strong positive feelings that tip the buyer into impulse mode (*The Psychology of Urgency*, 2018). On the other hand, negative emotions or a sense of overwhelm can pull them back and stall the close.

Common Buyer Emotions

Here's a quick breakdown of common buyer feelings as a close draws near:

- **Anticipation:** excitement about what's next if they say yes

- **Apprehension:** worries about wasting money, regret, or being pressured

- **Anxiety:** fear of missing out, but also fear of making the wrong choice

- **Relief:** the feeling that comes after they make the choice and the tension drops

You can spot these feelings in the language buyers use. When someone says things like "I just need a night to sleep on it" or "It sounds good, but I'm still not sure," they're feeling stuck between anticipation and apprehension. If a buyer asks, "What happens after I sign?" or "Can you remind me of the warranty?" it means they're close but still need reassurance.

In my vacuum-selling days, I watched that grandmother go through every single one of these emotions in the span of maybe 15 minutes.

The anticipation when she saw the sand demonstration, the apprehension when she heard the price, the anxiety about spending so much, and then—after that unexpected emotional moment—the relief that came with her decision. She wasn't just relieved to have a powerful vacuum; she was relieved to have reconnected with a cherished memory.

The Seller's Experience

The seller goes through their own rollercoaster of feelings. Right before the close, many sellers feel both hope and worry. Their confidence might surge as they sense the buyer's interest growing, but a sudden tough question can cause a dip. Sellers also feel a responsibility to guide the buyer well. The best sellers don't just want a signed contract—they want the buyer to feel good about saying yes. High-pressure tactics might work sometimes, but understanding where the buyer is emotionally is more effective in the long run (PwC, 2023).

I can tell you from experience, standing in that living room at 16 years old, watching tears stream down that woman's face, I felt everything: panic, confusion, empathy, hope—all at once. I wasn't thinking about my commission anymore. I was thinking about whether I'd somehow caused harm, whether I should apologize, whether I should just pack up and leave. The responsibility of that moment felt enormous, even if I couldn't have articulated it that way at the time.

Sellers watch for tells: Are buyers leaning in, making eye contact, taking notes? Are they fidgeting, glancing at doors, or making excuses to stall? Sellers use empathy and active listening to determine when to back off and when to push gently forward.

Making It Easy

On a practical level, the close relies on the seller's ability to lay out next steps in a way that feels easy and safe. This is where the transactional side comes in. Clear instructions, confirmation of details, and a written summary all help buyers feel less overwhelmed. Sellers might say, "If you're ready, I can get the paperwork started. Here's exactly what will happen next." This kind of language reassures buyers that they won't be lost once they say yes.

The deeper understanding here is that a close blends emotion with action. It isn't just about persuading someone—it's about building enough trust and confidence that both sides are ready to take a leap. Buyers aren't all the same. Some need more emotional support, while others look for practical reassurances.

Types of Closes and When to Use Them

Feelings often run high as a sales conversation nears the close. Buyers might be excited, hesitant, or just plain tired of talking, and every choice you make as a closer shapes their experience. Different closing techniques fit as naturally as slipping into your favorite pair of shoes. Some approaches keep the energy light and steady, others speed up the tempo, and some act like a gentle "no-pressure" nudge.

The Assumptive Close

The assumptive close is like talking to a friend and planning an outing, already expecting they'll say yes. In a retail setting, imagine a shopper lingering by a jacket, running their hand along the fabric. You might say, "Would you like me to ring this up or get it gift-wrapped for you?" You act as if the decision's already made—your words invite the buyer to join in, not debate the basics.

This works best when there's been plenty of agreement and positive signals along the way. Maybe the buyer has nodded, asked about delivery, or seems relaxed and open. People often go along when it feels like the next step is already in motion. The assumptive close increases confidence for both sides and helps push through lingering doubts without feeling pushy. It keeps the focus on "how" rather than "if" the purchase will happen. This technique fits best when connection and trust are strong, and it's clear that what you're offering meets the buyer's needs.

Looking back, I realize I was using elements of the assumptive close without even knowing it. When I asked to take off my tie and roll up my sleeves, I wasn't asking permission to leave—I was assuming we were moving forward with the demonstration. When I asked where a good place to vacuum would be, I wasn't asking whether she wanted to see the vacuum work—I assumed she did and just needed to pick a spot.

The Urgency Close

Sometimes, the moment demands more of a spark. The urgency close picks up the tempo by giving the buyer a deadline or a reason to act fast. You might tell a client, "This offer is here until Friday—after that, we can't guarantee these terms." Maybe there's a sale ending, limited stock, or a special incentive.

The urgency close works when buyers seem interested but slow to commit, maybe waiting for a sign to move forward. It lights a small fire, shifting the focus from endless consideration to immediate action. When urgency is genuine (not faked), it helps people make choices rather than put them off. Buyers who have a strong interest but tend to procrastinate or get distracted may benefit from this kind of nudge. Watch for cues like hesitation, questions about timelines, or comments about "thinking it over"—these signal that urgency might be the momentum shift you need.

The Summary Close

Feeling stuck in a cycle of questions and maybes? The summary close can break that loop. Here, you gently recap the main points you and the buyer have already agreed on. "Just to recap," you say, "we'll be handling delivery, setup, and your support is covered for the first six months. All that's left is to pick your color."

The summary close is helpful when buyers start to forget what they liked, get overwhelmed, or seem to lose track of why they were interested in the first place. It pulls together the conversation's best threads and shows that you've been listening. It also makes buyers feel cared for, because you're aligning what you're offering with what matters most to them (Gibbons, 2018). Subtle signals for this approach include buyers looking uncertain, repeating old concerns, or asking for reassurance about the benefits.

The Takeaway Close

Now and then, a conversation feels like it's going in circles, with buyers asking for more sweeteners, extra discounts, or "just one more thing." If they're dragging their feet despite all the value on the table, the takeaway close gives control back to the salesperson. You might say, "This package is the best we can do. If it's not the right fit, I don't want to waste your time."

Suddenly, instead of pushing the sale, you're gently offering to step away. Buyers who really want what you've shown will often snap back into focus. The surprise of possibly losing the chance changes the power dynamic; it feels genuine, not desperate. This close is most effective when buyers hesitate too long or use stalling tactics. Tune in to cues like repeated demands for extras or signaling they're thinking about walking away—these hint it's time for a takeaway. It works because people tend to want something more when they realize they might lose it.

Finding Your Style

Start thinking about which of these closes lines up with your natural strengths and everyday situations. If you like confident, natural conversations, the assumptive close might become your favorite move. If your context is more deal-driven or you deal with last-minute shoppers, urgency may serve you well. With complex sales, the summary close often shines. Negotiators who dislike endless wrangling may find the takeaway close freeing. Adjusting your close to fit the moment isn't about tricks; it's about reading signals and feeling out what the buyer needs next.

Recognizing and Responding to Buying Signals

Having the right closing line is only half the story. The other half is knowing when to use it, and that comes down to spotting buying signals. The small but unmistakable cues people give off during conversations—whether it's a question about price, a curious look down at your proposal, or a comment about how quickly a problem could be solved—are your signposts. Getting comfortable reading these signals makes assumption-based closing lines ring true and natural, not forced.

Verbal Buying Signals

Suppose you're chatting with a customer and they suddenly ask, "If we signed today, how soon would delivery happen?" Instantly, you know the conversation has shifted. They're not just weighing options; they're picturing how to use your solution.

Verbal cues carry a lot of meaning. Some prospects get down to brass tacks—asking about payment terms, contract length, or what previous customers thought of your guarantees. They may dig into details about why other clients canceled contracts or how you compare to a rival. These questions may feel challenging, but seasoned sales leaders know that this kind of "grilling" is actually a great sign. Someone who's not interested won't bother going that far; someone thinking of buying wants to be sure, so they probe, press, and imagine themselves as part of your world (*11 Buying Signals to Look*, n.d.).

When that grandmother asked me, "How much did you say the vacuum was?" after her emotional moment, that was a verbal buying signal I almost missed because I was so caught up in the shock of the situation. But looking back, the shift in her question—from "That's very expensive" to "How much did you say it was?"—signaled that something fundamental had changed in her mind.

Nonverbal Buying Signals

Nonverbal signals sometimes shout even louder than words. Picture someone who nudges the contract closer as you talk, taps it lightly, or relaxes their posture after you address an objection. These are nonverbal signals—a raised eyebrow, a nod, leaning in just a touch closer. Each of these is like a small green light, telling you the path is open for the next step (*11 Buying Signals to Look*, n.d.).

The buyer who suddenly starts to mirror your gestures, sits up straighter, or responds to your slides with an eager half-smile is likely moving toward yes. Maybe you spot them running a finger thoughtfully along the contract or glancing frequently at the price page. Body language can give you a read far before direct questions come up.

I remember watching that woman wipe her eyes and then look at the vacuum differently. Her body language shifted—she wasn't leaning away from it anymore, she was looking at it with something like gratitude. That nonverbal signal told me everything I needed to know, even if I was too young and inexperienced to fully recognize it at the time.

The Trap of Overselling

Acting when these signals show up is what sets effective closers apart. The biggest trap is overselling. Once the affirmative signs appear, the urge to keep pitching is powerful. You want to make extra sure to add one more benefit or overcome one last hypothetical objection. But that move often backfires. Instead of letting excitement build, you end up talking the customer right out of their decision.

Picture a salesperson who, after getting a "This sounds perfect, when can we start?" keeps talking about extra features or new updates. The prospect's smile starts to fade, the energy seeps out, and they end up needing more "time to think." The real lesson: When the signals say "ready," sometimes the most persuasive thing you can do is go quiet or ask, "Should we get this scheduled?"

I'm grateful that in my inexperience, I didn't oversell. I didn't launch into more features about the vacuum or try to justify the price again. I just stood there, probably looking terrified, and let the moment be what it was. Sometimes, not knowing the "advanced techniques" protects you from your own worst instincts.

Pushing past the close can also damage trust. Customers sense desperation instantly; what once felt like a partnership now seems pushy. It's a quick shift from excitement to doubt. Instead of locking in the win, you create second thoughts—just because you didn't recognize the moment to pause and let them come toward you.

Mindset of a Closer

When someone figures out how to spot buying signals—the little hints, nods, questions, or pauses that tell you a customer is right there on the edge of agreeing—the next move isn't about jumping in louder or trying to be clever. What happens inside your own head at that moment is just as important as reading the other person. That moment is where a closer's unique mindset starts to show. It's the difference between confidently stepping forward and making the call, or hanging back and letting uncertainty take over.

Confidence vs. Arrogance

Being a strong closer has nothing to do with being pushy. It's not about dazzling the room or dominating the conversation. What sets great closers apart is the quiet belief that they belong at the table and that their solutions have real value. They stand out not because they chase approval, but because they bring a sense of calm certainty to the whole process.

You can see this in the way they hold themselves. There's relaxed eye contact, open gestures, and a posture that communicates both attention and comfort—not bravado or swagger. This attitude also shows up in the words they use. A confident closer says things like, "Based on everything you've told me, this plan seems like a strong fit. How do you feel about getting started?" That's steady, honest, and focused on the customer's experience. Compare that with phrases dripping with arrogance, like, "You'd regret going with anyone else," or "It's obvious this is your only logical option." That's the sound of someone trying to hustle, not help.

The dividing line between confidence and arrogance can get blurry when the pressure is high. True confidence comes from preparation—knowing your product, your process, and your customer inside and out. It grows from regular practice, learning from wins and losses, and honest feedback. Arrogance, by contrast, feels hollow. It's often just a mask for insecurity, and it shows up when someone starts acting like the customer should feel lucky to even be at the table.

At 16, I had no business being confident. I barely knew what I was doing. But what I did have was a genuine belief that this vacuum was incredible—because it was. I'd seen it work. I'd watched it defy gravity with steel balls and sand. I knew it was worth the money, even if I couldn't articulate why in sophisticated sales language. That genuine belief carried me through, even when I wanted to run out the door.

Building the Right Mentality

Building a "I deserve this sale" mentality is about much more than pep talks. It's about stacking up daily choices and habits that cement your sense of worth. For one thing, preparation is non-negotiable. The more you invest in knowing what you're offering and how it genuinely solves problems, the easier it is to trust yourself in tough moments. Every time you review past notes, run practice conversations, or roleplay objections, you're building the foundation for the kind of confidence that wins respect—yours and the customer's.

Another solid practice is reflecting on real wins, no matter how small. Take time after those deals where everything clicked and look at what you did right. Maybe you listened with care, or you helped someone see an option they hadn't considered. Let those moments remind you that your skills are real and earned.

Self-Talk and Active Listening

Self-talk shapes the whole inner game of closing. A reliable closer talks to themselves the way a good coach would—encouraging, direct, and honest. Instead of feeding doubts ("What if they ask a question I can't answer?"), they flip the script: "I've handled tough questions before, and I can handle them again." If nerves creep in, they breathe deep and step back to what they know.

Active listening also plays a huge role. Listening closely isn't just about catching what's said; it's about picking up on tone, hesitations, and the things left unsaid. By showing customers they're heard and respected, you prove you don't have to oversell or rush. When objections pop up, a confident closer stays steady: "I appreciate your concern. Let's walk through that together." If a deal falls apart, they focus on what they can learn and move forward without blaming the customer or themselves.

I had no formal training in active listening back then, but I knew enough to shut up when someone was crying. I knew enough to let the moment breathe. Sometimes, the most valuable sales skill is just being human—being present with someone in their experience, whatever that experience happens to be.

Staying Humble

Catch yourself when confidence slips into arrogance by asking a simple question: *Am I serving or am I performing?* If you feel the urge to talk over the customer, push for quick answers, or show off knowledge, it's time to step back. Practice humility by admitting what you don't know. When you're not pretending to have all the answers, genuine trust follows. A great closer shines by being present, prepared, and truly believing the solution is the right one—for the customer and for themselves.

The truth is, that sale humbled me. It showed me that I didn't control anything—not really. I couldn't have scripted that moment if I'd tried. All I could do was show up, do my demonstration honestly, and be present for whatever happened next. That's a lesson that's served me far beyond that single vacuum sale.

Wrapping It Up

That vacuum sale taught me something I've never forgotten: People buy on emotion—happy, sad, shocked, nostalgic, it doesn't matter. Emotion sells. The vacuum didn't just clean that woman's carpet; it cleaned her soul. I didn't just sell a vacuum that day. I sold peace of mind, closure, and the removal of a decade-old dog imprint.

With practice, you'll start to feel that natural rhythm where talking less sometimes means winning more, and where trust leads the way to yes. You'll learn to recognize when a demonstration has done its work, when the signals are all pointing in the right direction, and when the best thing you can do is simply ask for the sale and then be quiet.

So, let's take these insights forward, sharpen our instincts, and get ready to close with a calm, confident style that turns conversations into connections—and connections into lasting wins. Remember: The close isn't about manipulation or pressure. It's about being present, being genuine, and recognizing those moments when emotion and logic align to create a decision that serves everyone involved.

Chapter 6:
The Art of the Voice

"Can you hear the doubt in my voice?" a client once asked me during a call. It caught me off guard because I thought my words were clear and confident. But that moment stuck with me—how much more people pick up from how we say things, not just what we say.

I've spent years on sales floors, listening to thousands of calls, coaching reps who couldn't figure out why their pitches weren't landing. And I kept coming back to the same truth: Your voice is your power. A stronger voice creates authority. Authority creates trust. Trust creates sales. It's that simple, and that profound.

Have you ever noticed how someone's tone can make you feel instantly at ease or on edge? Or how your own voice shifts when you're nervous or excited? We all carry a powerful tool in our voices, whether we realize it or not, and learning to use it well can change the way people listen, trust, and respond.

What if your voice was more than just sound? What if it was the secret weapon in your sales toolkit? Let me show you how your voice sets the stage for every conversation before a single word truly lands.

Why Voice Is More Powerful Than Words

People remember how you sound even more than what you say. In sales, the right voice can do more than simply share information; it draws people in, keeps them listening, and opens the door to trust.

The Science Behind Vocal Impact

Research like Albert Mehrabian's famous communication model helps explain this. When people try to decide if a message is sincere, only about 7% comes from the actual words, while 38% comes from tone and 55% from body language (Carrier, 2019). Even without seeing someone face-to-face, your vocal tone still shapes those snap impressions. No matter how good your pitch, if your voice quivers or sounds flat, people can sense uncertainty, doubt, or lack of genuine interest long before you finish your first sentence.

Consider picking up the phone and hearing a monotone greeting: "Hello, how can I help you today?" Spoken in a lifeless drone, even the best offer runs into a wall. Now, imagine a spark in the voice: "Hi! Thanks for calling! What can I do for you today?" The difference jumps out before the words register. One delivers an invisible yawn, the other a boost of energy.

The Phone Steals Your Energy

Here's something I learned the hard way, and it changed everything about how I approach calls: Over the phone, you lose about 40% of your natural tone, emotion, and energy. Forty percent. That means the enthusiasm you think you're projecting? It's landing as lukewarm at best. The confidence you feel? It's coming across as uncertainty.

I discovered this when I started recording my own calls and playing them back. I thought I sounded engaged and dynamic. What I actually heard was someone who sounded half-asleep. It was humbling, and it was exactly the wake-up call I needed.

The top reps I've worked with all figured this out. They compensate by being louder—more authoritative, clearer, stronger. Not yelling. Not being rude. But projecting confidence in a way that cuts through the limitations of the medium. They understand that what feels like "too much" energy in the moment often lands as "just right" on the other end of the line.

Emotional Contagion in Action

Buyers, friends, and even total strangers pick up on these subtle signals, often adjusting their mood in response. This is emotional contagion. When someone's voice carries energy, hope, or excitement, those feelings can bounce right into the listener's experience. It's as if tone hands over an emotional baton they want to grab.

Think about times when someone's enthusiasm made you start to feel confident or curious before you even understood what they were talking about. Maybe a manager rallied the team before a challenging project, and the group started believing in the plan almost on cue—not just because of the message, but because of the leader's tone. Or maybe a friend's laughter over the phone lifted your mood before you shared any news of your own.

In sales, the same effect works both ways. That first "Good morning!" packed with authentic warmth can lower defenses. On the other hand, a flat, mechanical voice can close off the conversation, tell people, "This isn't worth your energy," and make every next sentence harder to land.

I remember coaching a rep named Marcus who had all the product knowledge in the world but couldn't close to save his life. When I listened to his calls, I immediately understood why. His voice was thin, hesitant, almost apologetic. He sounded like he was asking permission to exist. We worked on projecting authority—not arrogance, but genuine confidence. Within three weeks, his close rate doubled. Same words, same product, same market. Different voice.

The Five Levers of Tone

What goes into tone? There are five levers you can pull: pitch, pace, inflection, volume, and pauses that let key ideas settle.

- Pitch operates on a spectrum. A higher pitch can signal excitement or, sometimes, nervousness. A lower pitch might sound calming and trustworthy, or it might slip into dullness if you're not careful. I tend to drop my pitch slightly when I'm making an important point—it signals gravity and draws the listener in.

- Pace is where many reps go wrong. Racing through sentences can sound nervous or rushed, sometimes leaving listeners behind. Slow down too much and the message starts to drag, risking boredom. The sweet spot is conversational but purposeful—like you have somewhere to go but you're not running from anything.

- Inflection turns a statement into a question or injects surprise and energy into a story. People naturally pay attention to the music in speech, not just its meaning. Flat inflection is the enemy of engagement.

- Volume can express strength or urgency. Soften it, and the voice becomes gentle or soothing. Get too loud, and it might come across as aggressive. But here's the key insight I want you to remember: Most people err on the side of too quiet, especially over the phone. That 40% energy loss I mentioned? Volume is how you get it back.

- Pauses create a moment of silence to let your listener reflect, build suspense, or draw a mental spotlight to what comes next. I'll dive deeper into this shortly because it's one of the most underused tools in a salesperson's arsenal.

Practice Observation Exercise

Try turning these ideas into real-world practice. Next time you walk into a coffee shop, bank, or any checkout line, pay attention to the people ahead of you. Does the cashier's enthusiasm spread a little warmth through the queue, or does a bored response pass that feeling down the line? On the phone, in meetings, or even at home, notice what grabs your ear first. Often, it's not facts or details but a hint of mood, attitude, or openness that comes through in a person's sound.

Matching and Adapting Your Voice

In sales, learning to listen for these clues is just as important as what you say. When you hear excitement or joy, match that spark and run with it. Raise your energy and let the conversation build. If you hear hesitation, slow your delivery, clarify, or gently ask what's on their mind. When you notice skepticism or tightness, lower your tone, soften your inflection, and offer a listening ear.

Each of these moves helps keep the conversation alive and, more importantly, makes the listener feel understood.

Get curious for a day and listen for these patterns everywhere you go. You'll start to spot just how much tone controls the direction of talk, sways emotions, or opens doors before content ever gets a chance. Knowing this first step sets up every other vocal skill, because interpreting the world's sounds sharpens your ability to shape your own. Mastering your delivery comes next. It means playing with these tools so your own voice becomes a steady guide—not just talking, but leaving people feeling seen, heard, and ready to engage.

Practicing Inflection, Pace, and Pause

It all starts with simple, hands-on practice using tools you already have. Imagine grabbing your phone or opening a computer app and recording yourself during a pitch or sample sales call. This isn't about being perfect the first time. It's about listening for what's really going on in your delivery.

The Power of Recording Yourself

Maybe you catch yourself racing through details at the start or realize your tone flattens out just as you try to close. Practice offers an honest mirror, revealing habits that go unnoticed when you're speaking in real time (Academy, 2025).

When you listen back, you start to notice patterns: energy that fizzles halfway through, a sing-songy rhythm that makes you sound less sincere, or plowing through pauses that should let your message sink in.

I'll never forget the first time I recorded myself and played it back. I was three years into my sales career and thought I had it figured out. What I heard was someone who spoke too fast, swallowed the ends of sentences, and had this nervous laugh that punctuated every third statement. It was painful to listen to. It was also the most valuable 30 minutes I ever spent on self-improvement.

Take someone who always lowers their voice and speeds up as soon as pricing is mentioned. The recording makes that moment jump out, making it easy to spot and fix.

Loop and Improve

This is why looping over sticky sections matters. If your energy drops right before you ask for the meeting, re-record that bit with extra animation or a well-timed pause. The next time, play with pitch. Maybe bringing your tone up just before you pose the question. Let yourself exaggerate on purpose, then scale back until it feels natural. The change in energy and rhythm will not only be audible but will feel comfortable, giving you extra confidence with each attempt (Academy, 2025).

Mastering the Pause

Pause control is a true game-changer that brings authority and gets listeners leaning in. Think of those scenes in movies when everything goes quiet—a long pause builds suspense right before the most important line. In real life, most new salespeople rush and stuff their points into one breath. But when you practice hitting "pause" after a key question, your words land with much more impact.

Compare these two approaches:

- **With pauses:** "With this plan, your team can save hours... every week... Would that make a difference for you?" (pause)

- **Without pauses:** "With this plan your team can save hours every week would that make a difference for you?"

The first example gives the listener space to think. You command the conversation and show that what's coming is worth hearing. Pauses are not just for drama; they're for clarity, for effect, for letting the person on the other end digest your point.

Adding intention to pauses takes practice, but it pays off. Next time you practice, pick a place in your script for a deliberate silent beat. Count "one-one-thousand" to yourself, and listen to the difference. The awkwardness fades with repetition, and soon that silence becomes your ally.

Step-By-Step Practice Protocol

Detailed steps make progress easy to track and repeat. Here's the protocol I developed over years of coaching:

1. Record your baseline. Open your phone or computer and record a two-minute pitch, conversation, or voicemail intro. Don't aim for perfection—focus on natural delivery.

2. Do an active listening review. Find a quiet place, play back your recording, and listen for tone, energy, and pauses. Jot down spots where your voice feels forced, your energy sags, or you ramble through key points.

3. Identify improvement targets. Choose three things to improve, like too many filler words, lack of pitch change, or not enough pauses after important statements.

4. Practice with exaggeration. Record the same segment, this time exaggerating vocal variety. Go bigger with changes in pitch, slow down for emphasis, and add intentional pauses. This feels ridiculous at first. Do it anyway.

5. Refine daily. Repeat this exercise daily for a week. Each time, review your list of habits, mark changes, and celebrate any noticeable growth in confidence or clarity.

Salespeople who master these basics come across as more poised and trustworthy, keeping listeners with them every step of the way (Academy, 2025). Deliberate recording and playback put you directly in touch with your progress—no guesswork, no waiting for outside feedback.

Beyond Technique to Confidence

Developing this vocal control is about more than technique. Sellers quickly discover that gaining command over their pace, tone, and pauses changes how they feel about challenging calls. They stand taller—literally and figuratively—projecting belief in every word. This sense of control frees you up to focus on connection, not performance (Academy, 2025).

Remember: A stronger voice creates authority. Authority creates trust. Trust creates sales. Every minute you spend developing your vocal presence pays dividends across every conversation you'll ever have.

Sounding Confident When Nervous

Every reader who's tried recording and replaying their voice, or deliberately pausing mid-pitch, has already taken solid steps toward building a more controlled sound. With control comes another big motivation—wanting to sound confident, even when nervous energy bubbles right under the surface.

Walking into a call, meeting, or sales conversation with calm confidence creates a magnetic presence. That presence isn't luck or natural talent. It starts before a single word, with rituals that ground both body and mind.

The Foundation: Breathing Techniques

I developed my pre-call routine after a particularly brutal stretch where I bombed five major presentations in a row. My voice was tight, my breathing shallow, and I could hear the desperation in my own tone. Something had to change.

Imagine the moment right before a big call: a hand pressed against the chest, quietly inhaling and exhaling, feeling excitement and nerves mix together. Here's the exercise that saved my career: 4-6 breathing. To try it out, draw in a breath through your nose, counting to four. Feel your belly rise more than your chest. Part your lips and let the air flow out slowly while counting to six. Repeat the whole cycle three or four times.

As you exhale, notice your shoulders dropping and your throat relaxing. This breathing technique slows heart rate and gives your body a cue to switch gears, making your voice less likely to shake (Bordo et al., 2025). Over time, you'll notice your sound settling into a steadier, richer place, acting like an anchor when pressure rises.

Posture: Your Physical Foundation

As breath flows more easily, posture steps in to multiply the confidence effect. Picture how you would sound slouched in a chair—shoulders rounded, body caved inward. Now, visualize standing with both feet flat, shoulders drawn gently back, and chin lifted, as if someone's pulling a string from the top of your head.

This "golden string" image straightens your spine and strengthens your core, creating space for breath and quickly making your voice sound more commanding.

Try it in a chair, too: Scoot forward, plant your feet, roll your shoulders back, and lift your head. Read out loud or dial into a call from this posture, and notice how much more robust and energized your sound feels. Posture isn't about looking stiff; it's about building a channel between your lungs, throat, and mouth that supports both breath and words (García-Monge et al., 2023).

I stand for every important call now. Even when I'm working from home, even when no one can see me. The difference in my voice is *that* significant.

Mental Rehearsal: Visualization

More than just the body, truly projecting confidence draws from mental rehearsal—the art of visualization. Take a moment before each conversation to find a quiet space and close your eyes. Breathe deep and picture yourself greeting the client in a calm, steady tone. See their face as they nod along, engaged and interested. Hold onto that image for at least 10 seconds. If your brain tries to sneak in a nervous thought, gently bring the picture back to what you want: a relaxed voice, a positive connection, a smooth interaction.

Training your mind to see a positive outcome rewires your memory, calming the cycle of worry and priming both your voice and your body for confidence. Practicing this step crafts a mental "script" of success and helps switch anxious anticipation to excitement or readiness (García-Monge et al., 2023).

Pre-Call Rituals That Work

Pre-call jitters are as normal as the urge to triple-check your notes. Some might feel their throat tighten or their hands begin to sweat a little as a meeting approaches. To head off those nerves, I use a few physical reset techniques.

Cold water works wonders—sip slowly to loosen your vocal cords. Fist-clenching helps, too: Clench your fists under the table, hold for five seconds, then release to push the reset on tension. A quick shake of the hands under your desk or behind your back clears out leftover jitters.

Sports come to mind here: athletes don't expect to enter competition cold. They warm up, stretch, and breathe, making performance a continuation of preparation instead of a sudden leap. Adopting a short pre-call routine can quiet nerves and cue your brain that it's game time.

Building a go-to routine helps pressure moments feel familiar. Over time, these techniques become associated with positive, calm outcomes. The key is to keep the rituals short but reliable. Even top sales professionals and performers have small behaviors or mantras they fall back on, whether that's a deep inhalation before the phone rings or a shoulder roll before a presentation (Bordo et al., 2025).

Hearing as an Extra Sense

Picture yourself in the middle of a high-stakes sales call. You have done all the warmup—steady breathing, strong posture, and a clear focus on your message. Now, you are on the line, and you realize that what gives your pitch the edge is not only how you sound, but how much you can hear.

Beyond Passive Hearing

Listening is more than letting sound hit your ears. It is your active radar for what the client is saying, how they feel, and even what they are not saying aloud. The moment you focus outward with intent, you pick up insights that a simple script cannot reveal.

A passive listener hears: "That all sounds fine. I'll think it over." An active listener notices the pause, the slight dip at "fine," and an undercurrent that hints at doubt or reluctance.

Passive hearing is a default state—background music at a café, voices in a crowded room, or sales chatter that does not register past the words. In contrast, active listening transforms the call. You lock in, direct your full attention to the client, and let distractions fade out, much like tuning a radio dial to capture the clearest signal.

Reading Between the Lines

Sales conversations are loaded with clues beneath the surface. A client who speaks rapidly at first, then slows down and adds, "I just need to check with my manager..." might be stalling for time, hinting at uncertainty, or bracing for conflict over budget approval.

Listen for vocal shifts. Does their tone change when money comes up? A light, upbeat tone that drops to flatness? A sudden sigh? Notice patterns: Are they repeating your words back, echoing concerns, or going silent at key moments?

Silence isn't nothing. It may signal that your client just got overwhelmed or that they are weighing a question carefully. Jumping in too fast can break the moment; letting the silence breathe shows respect and gives space for truth to surface.

Active Listening in Practice

Active listening needs a real plan, not just good intentions. It means listening all the way through before responding. It means keeping your mind from racing ahead to the next bullet point, and instead reflecting what you just heard.

The paraphrase technique is powerful: "So, what I'm hearing is that timing is the biggest concern right now—is that right?"

This not only checks your understanding, but it also signals the client that you care about the details of their world (Cabuyao, 2023). In the heat of a sales moment, it is tempting to jump to a solution or defend your offer, but that can shut down trust fast. Stay focused, avoid reacting out of habit, and remember the two-way flow of conversation.

Listening Skills Exercise

Try this exercise to boost your active listening muscle. After your next real or practice call, replay the recording in 60-second segments. Write down not just the words, but every sigh, laugh, moment of silence, and shift in pace or emphasis. Note how the client sounded when they brought up cost, timing, or when you gave them an option. Identify what feelings might be running under their words: interest, worry, excitement, or hesitation.

In role-plays or even casual conversations, try mirroring the emotional tone you hear. If your client or friend sounds apprehensive, respond with a gentle, steady voice. If they brighten, allow your voice to lift too. This breaks down barriers and helps create a sense of safety and understanding (Hazy et al., 2015).

Keep an ear out for the difference between reacting and responding. Reacting means you are on autopilot—answering the surface question, rushing to fill a pause. Responding means you pause, process what was shared, and reply with care.

Using Assertiveness to Tip the Scale

Sometimes, the first signal that a sales conversation is changing happens long before anything is said outright. You might notice a longer-than-usual pause, a sudden quietness, or even a shift in the client's energy. Recognizing these moments means you've been putting into practice the active listening and emotional awareness covered earlier.

What Is Controlled Assertiveness?

Controlled assertiveness is the tool that lets you steer these moments with confidence. Picture an everyday sales call. The client interrupts you for the third time, their tone clipped, showing impatience.

The unskilled reaction is to tighten your voice, speed up your words, and start restating your pitch, hoping to force your message through. This only signals desperation and causes further resistance.

The controlled assertiveness response sounds like this: "I want to make sure I'm addressing what matters most to you. Can we revisit your priorities?"

The voice stays relaxed, the pace steady, and the underlying message is one of confidence and respect.

Controlled assertiveness means you hold your ground without aggression or neediness. You don't shy away from difficult moments, nor do you give in every time there's a bump in the conversation. This approach shares similarities with the "collaborating" and "compromising" strategies mentioned in conflict management research. Choosing to collaborate—looking for a win-win outcome—often starts with using a composed voice that opens doors rather than closes them (Corona, 2025).

Two Key Scenarios

Sales conversations are full of choices about when to speak up and when to lean back.

In the first scenario, you're pushing forward the right way. Your client seems hesitant, so you say: "Would you be open to sharing what's holding you back?" The way you deliver this question matters as much as the question itself. If your voice rises at the end, tight from tension, it suggests anxiety. When you say it in a warm, measured voice, you invite honesty and keep the door open.

In the second scenario, you're pulling back. Maybe you sense irritation from the client, or maybe their answers grow short. Instead of pressing harder, you soften your tone: "Perhaps this isn't the right fit at the moment, and that's okay."

This moment of stepping back can de-escalate tension and shows that your confidence isn't tied to a quick sale. You project the same balanced, clear presence found in leaders who resolve conflict with empathy and patience, not with volume (*Difficult Conversations*,2023).

Practice Protocol for Poise

Practicing this poise starts with reflection. Recall a recent sales call where you sensed resistance. Replay the moment in your mind, focusing just on your delivery—the speed, the pitch, the way your voice landed. Consider whether you sounded steady or if your tone betrayed nerves.

Script one line you wish you had said, such as: "I want to be respectful of your time. If now isn't right, I'm happy to reconnect another day." Then, practice saying this line out loud, slowly and evenly, until you feel its calm authority in your body.

I've seen this transform reps who struggled with confrontational prospects. One manager I coached described how, after being interrupted repeatedly, he paused, recentered, and said: "Let's get back to your main priorities so I can be sure I'm helping you," in a tone that was both firm and caring. The client's demeanor changed; they felt heard, and a path to resolution opened.

The Quick Self-Check

You can instantly check your tone by asking yourself: *Would I want to listen to me right now?*

This simple mental check cuts through habits and helps keep your delivery aligned with true confidence.

Controlled assertiveness doesn't only show up when you're defending your offer or winning over objections. It's woven into every conversation, big and small. Whether you're setting boundaries, pausing to let the other side think, or speaking up with tough truths, your steady tone tells clients that you believe in your product and in yourself, without overpowering or chasing anyone (*Difficult Conversations*, 2023).

Wrapping It Up

Remember the core truth: A stronger voice creates authority. Authority creates trust. Trust creates sales. This isn't about becoming someone you're not. It's about removing the barriers between your genuine confidence and how that confidence lands with others.

You've seen how tuning in to others' tones helps guide your response and keeps conversations flowing smoothly. You've learned that over the phone, you're fighting against a 40% loss in natural energy, and now you know how to compensate. With practice, your voice will not just carry information but spark feeling, trust, and confidence in every interaction.

So, grab your phone, start recording, and listen closely. You're on the path to mastering a steady, confident sound that draws people in and opens doors, no matter what the next call or meeting throws your way.

Chapter 7:
Reading the Room

Have you ever walked into a room and felt like there was an invisible conversation happening before anyone said a word? Maybe someone shifted in their seat, avoided eye contact, or gave you a quick nod that said more than words ever could. Those moments are packed with signals—small clues about how people are feeling and what they might be thinking beneath the surface.

I remember experiencing this vividly early in my career. I'd walk into a meeting and sense tension before a single word was spoken. Someone's jaw would tighten. Another person would angle their body toward the door. These weren't random movements; they were messages, if you knew how to read them.

This chapter will take you behind the scenes of those silent exchanges, showing you how to pick up on body language, facial expressions, and energy levels. You'll learn how tuning into these subtle hints can change the way your sales conversations flow, helping you connect better, respond smarter, and ultimately build trust without saying a thing.

Reading Body Language: Universal Cues

A sales conversation starts before anyone says a word. When you walk into a meeting, there's immediate silent chatter—people shifting in their seats, folding or unfolding arms, glancing around the room. I've learned to get ahead by reading that silent dialogue and letting it shape how I approach the first question, the first story, even my opening smile.

Signs of Interest

Start with what shows you straight away that someone's interested. A client leaning toward you, keeping their shoulders open, nodding as you talk—these are golden signs. They're telling you, without risking a word, that your message is landing. The nod isn't just politeness. Watch for steady, gentle nodding—the kind that matches your own pace. It means your ideas are clicking, or at least your client is with you for this part of the ride.

Eye contact plays its role here. Frequent, sustained eye contact (minus the stare-down) signals engagement and honesty. This person probably wants more detail or is warming up to your pitch. You can let this boost your confidence and edge a little closer to closing, maybe asking questions that pull your client in deeper or offering more specific solutions. Remember, this is not just a hunch; it's informed by how nonverbal behaviors influence others, even if these signals don't work quite like formal language.

Defensive Signals

Now, imagine you're explaining your big value proposition, and your client suddenly shifts in their chair, forehead wrinkling, lips pressed a little tighter than before. Maybe their arms come up and cross just under their chest. That defensive posture flashes a simple message: "I've hit a bump." Often, this is paired with brief side glances, maybe at a notepad, a phone, or even just off to a far wall.

If you see this combination—furrowed brow, hesitant gaze, crossed arms—it's your cue that something you said didn't quite land. Reading these signals gives you the opportunity to pause, ask if there's any confusion or hesitation, and invite fresh questions instead of barreling ahead. This nimbleness comes from developed emotional intelligence. Staying tuned into these signals increases your self-awareness. You notice your own impulse to push or retreat, and instead you choose a path that supports a real conversation, not just a rehearsed presentation.

94

As I discussed in Chapter 2, when I was selling perfume as a 17-year-old kid, I learned quickly that recognizing emotional cues in real time wasn't optional—it was survival. A customer's face would cloud over, their posture would stiffen, and if I didn't catch that shift immediately, the sale was already lost. Quick emotional intelligence and improvisation became second nature. I discovered that turning people's anger into empathy was possible if you paid attention to what their bodies were telling you before their words caught up.

Disengagement Cues

Every sales pro faces the wall: signs of rejection. These are the cues you spot with an anxious gut. Think about a prospect who glances at the door every couple of minutes, starts collecting their things before the sit-down is finished, or suddenly fidgets with a pen or phone. The body is trying to exit, saying "I'm out," before the mouth ever admits it.

These are not the moments to swoop in and force a close. Instead, recognizing a cluster of these disengagement cues suggests you gracefully shift gears. Maybe you check in gently about timing, or you take a strategic pause to reassess rather than desperately hammering home benefits that aren't landing. Sometimes, leaving space for the client to speak or even suggesting a follow-up works better. Sales success thrives on understanding when to slow down, not just when to speed up.

Reading Patterns, Not Single Cues

It's tempting to overanalyze every twitch, but relying on just one nonverbal cue risks misunderstanding. A single crossed arm could simply mean your client's cold, not suspicious. Look for patterns. When you see a genuine smile paired with relaxed posture and easy eye contact, you probably have rapport. But if a forced smile is paired with stiff shoulders and restless tapping, skepticism might be simmering just under the surface. Patterns tell the real story—body language works best in clusters.

Culture and personality matter, too. Not everyone gestures with wild hands or nods the same way. A quick nod or a reserved glance may be all it takes to express interest, depending on where someone's from or their personality. Recognizing these individual differences keeps your read accurate and respectful.

Reading Body Language: Micro-Expressions and Gestures

Micro-expressions are the briefest flickers of emotion across a person's face. They last less than half a second and, in sales conversations, can leak a customer's real feelings mid-negotiation. Imagine talking price and, for a heartbeat, the customer's eyebrows lower and lips press tight. A split-second scowl or a flash of surprise appears, gone before most people even know to look for it.

What Micro-Expressions Reveal

These flashes can signal tension, excitement, or internal conflict—like a moment of doubt when an offer is on the table or a spark of interest just before someone asks about next steps. The key is remembering that these tiny signals aren't easy to spot. Most people, unless trained, only catch them by accident.

As I explained in Chapter 4, learning to spot nostalgia, grief, and surprise in a customer's face changed everything for me. I still remember the woman who came in looking at an expensive piece—a $2,500 item that, on paper, made no sense for her budget. But I watched her face as she handled it. There was something there, a softening around her eyes, a slight tremor in her hands.

She wasn't seeing the product in front of her. She was reliving a decade-old bond with her late pet. That moment of recognition—understanding that she was processing grief and memory, not making a rational purchase decision—allowed me to adjust my tone to match her emotional state. I spoke more softly. I gave her space. I didn't push.

She bought that $2,500 piece, and I learned that the real sale often happens in the emotional undercurrent, not the logical argument.

Micro-expressions can be masked by broader, more obvious emotions. Your customer might be smiling politely, but their eyes go wide as soon as you mention a delivery delay. Or they might let out a quick, involuntary frown in the middle of a sentence, paired with upbeat talk. Macro-expressions—those full, clear smiles or frowns we all know—tend to dominate the show, but look for little mismatches: a face that lights up while the eyes flash worry, or enthusiasm paired with a flare of the nostrils (Soni, 2025).

In fast-paced sales, those partial leaks often reveal the hesitation or excitement your pitch has caused. Brief downward glances, rapid eye blinks, or even a tiny tightening at the jaw can sneak in beneath a calm exterior—offering a window into how things are really going.

Hand Gestures as Communication

Hand gestures bring another set of clues, often carrying social meaning even when they seem casual. An open palm might look relaxed, but in this context, it can signal a customer's willingness to connect or share information. Palms facing upward tend to invite conversation. On the other side, hands tucked under a table, clenched into fists, or repeatedly balled and released may hint at discomfort or resistance. People sometimes tap their fingers when impatient, or drum them softly while thinking through options.

Let's consider a sales moment with concrete hand cues. You ask a direct question, and the client's fingers tap once, then stop. Their gaze drops briefly to their lap, then they bring their hand to their chin. This mix could signal they're weighing a tough decision. A different client asked the same question, lapses into stillness with both hands hidden—maybe they're feeling out of their depth. These moments matter, but keep in mind that the meaning of gestures relies on context.

Context Is Everything

Avoid leaping to conclusions based solely on a gesture or a fleeting facial flicker. Nonverbal cues always occur within a larger story: tone, words, past conversations, expectations, and the overall mood. If two clients both fidget with their pen, one might be nervous about money, the other only cold. Ask a soft, open-ended question to check your hunches. "How does that sound to you?" gives people space to reveal what their nonverbals may have hinted.

Someone might mask their true mood with a macro-expression—a long, steady smile—while a quick muscle flick betrays disappointment as price is revealed. Disguise behaviors, like sudden eye blinks or changes in gaze, often pop up alongside genuine feelings, especially when pressure builds. Check for clusters: Does a closed fist come with a lip press, or is it paired with relaxed shoulders? Watching both the face and the hands provides a more balanced read (Soni, 2025).

Energy Matching: Building Rapport Without Mimicry

Every sales meeting starts with an energy. When you walk into a room, the vibe is already there—the rhythm of voices, how quickly people respond, whether someone's gestures are flying or their arms are crossed and still. Even breathing and posture tell a story.

Understanding Energy Matching

Imagine you're sitting across from a client who grips their coffee, leans in with a big, animated smile, and peppers you with rapid-fire questions. Matching their mood, just a little, makes the space feel easy. Another time, your partner's shoulders slouch, their voice comes out softer, and their hands are folded on the table. Here, ramping down your own animation helps both of you relax. Tuning in to where others naturally "are" lets you adjust in real time, making it feel like you're on the same team.

This directly connects to what I shared in Chapter 4 about adjusting your tone to match the buyer's emotional state. When that grieving woman stood before me, contemplating a purchase wrapped up in memory and loss, I didn't maintain my usual upbeat energy. I dialed everything down: my voice, my gestures, my pace. I met her where she was emotionally, and that's when the real connection happened.

Matching energy is not acting or pretending. It's about catching the underlying pace and volume around you, then adjusting your own. It's subtle: If someone talks fast and laughs often, up your own expressiveness just enough to show you're present. If someone speaks softly and uses few gestures, let your own movements settle. The idea isn't to copy what your partner is doing but to glide into a rhythm together, so they feel safe and seen.

Exercise: Energy-Matching in Steps

1. The next time you enter a conversation, glance at your partner and rate their energy level on a scale of 1–5. A 1 means quiet, reserved, slow-paced; a 5 means high-energy, talkative, expressive.

2. Notice three things: the way they hold their body (tense or loose, leaning in or back), their facial expressiveness (lots of smiles or neutral), and the speed and volume of their speech.

3. Choose one thing to adjust in yourself—your voice, facial expression, or posture.

4. Match their energy one step closer, not mirror it exactly.

5. Watch for changes: Does the conversation flow more easily? Does your partner warm up or look more at ease?

Small shifts matter. If someone is anxious and closed off, crossing your own legs and softening your shoulders helps. With an outgoing customer, smile brighter and raise your voice a notch. These changes build a sense of comfort—without awkwardness.

Avoiding the "Mimicry Trap"

There's one big warning sign to watch for: Forced or overt copying can backfire. If you instantly mimic a hand gesture or repeat a laugh, the person in front of you may notice, and it might make them pull away. You want them to feel joined, not mocked.

To avoid mimicry, use a time delay: if you notice a relaxed position, wait a moment before shifting into it, rather than copying straight away. Blend mirroring with your own response: If they sit back and sigh, you might relax your arms but keep your voice steady instead of giving a big sigh yourself. Focus on the bigger "energy" rather than each small gesture. Notice their overall rhythm. Do they joke, keep it light, or are they slow and serious?

Imagine this scenario: You're chatting about a product. The client scratches their chin; ten seconds later, you do too, thinking it shows empathy. The client sees it and goes quiet, even sits back in their chair. That's the moment mimicry turned into awkwardness. The smoother approach: Notice their laid-back tone, and a minute later, you relax your own posture, signaling subtle agreement rather than playing copycat.

Signs of Rapport

Reliable indicators that rapport is forming pop up in many ways: Eye contact gets more prolonged and more frequent, smiles feel warmer (not just polite), both people relax—shoulders drop, voices soften or gain energy together—and your partner may start matching your energy in small ways, too.

Energy-matching isn't about "winning" the conversation. It changes as the talk goes on. Take moments to check in with yourself. Is your partner opening up? Maybe now it helps to move a bit closer to their speed or add a new burst of warmth.

Mirroring Techniques: Verbal Mirroring and Pacing

Building off the confidence you've built reading energy and matching nonverbal cues, you can tap into verbal mirroring for next-level connection. Instead of relying only on body language or posture, you start tuning into the music of language itself. Every conversation carries its own rhythm, favorite words, and even pauses that act like a signature.

The Art of Verbal Mirroring

By listening this closely—and responding in kind—you create a comforting loop the other person feels almost instantly. People feel seen when you echo their word choices or speech style, not just their laughter or posture across a table.

This isn't about parroting back whatever's said. It's about catching those little flourishes—a turn of phrase, a nickname for a service, a repeated metaphor—that person uses to share what matters most. Say you're in a pitch, and your client says, "Let's make this project bulletproof." That's not just wishful thinking; it reveals how they want to feel about the end result. Later in the meeting, you could say, "That'll go a long way toward keeping things bulletproof." The echo isn't random; it confirms you're on the same page, and the client relaxes, trusting that you've caught the vibe they want to create.

I think back to my teenage years at the perfume counter, as I described in Chapter 2. I didn't have fancy training or sales methodology. What I had was the instinct to listen—really listen—to how customers talked about what they wanted. If a woman described wanting to smell "sophisticated but not old," I'd use those exact words when presenting options. If a man said he wanted something "clean, not too much," I'd echo that language back. This verbal mirroring, combined with quick emotional intelligence and improvisation, built human connection as a sales tool more powerful than any technique I'd learn later in formal training.

The Power of Active Listening

The secret ingredient is listening—even under pressure, even when you've got points to make. Avoid planning your next words, and let your focus drift to the speaker's vocabulary, the way they shape their sentences, the ramping up or quieting down of their tone. If they use formal words, you can pull your own speech in that direction. If they switch to something playful or casual, your replies can match the mood.

Matching Pace

Matching pace isn't about talking fast just because the other person is. Tune into the tempo. A person who sits quietly and answers thoughtfully deserves a bit of silence before you reply. Rushing in breaks their vibe. On the flip side, a high-energy chat needs light, fast back-and-forth. The beauty is in the soft shadows: Lean into the way you pause, change volume, or hold back a second to breathe with your partner in conversation (Carrier, 2019).

Setting Boundaries

Boundaries matter. If mirroring feels like a game of copycat, you've gone too far. It's about a gentle resemblance, not mimicry or mockery. Only pick up the parts that feel natural to you, leaving room for authenticity. The goal is to build trust—not to make someone uncomfortable or seen through. That starts with intention: Mirror only those things that come up naturally, like key phrases, a gentle laugh, or a noticeable long pause.

Practical Application

Let's make it practical. Think about how you could try this out today. Start with the next conversation at work or over coffee. Listen for three things the other person repeats, whether it's a quirky phrase, the way they greet you, or the speed at which they wrap up their thoughts.

Let's say you notice someone always says, "At the end of the day..." before sharing their opinion. When the discussion shifts, try using that phrase yourself: "At the end of the day, everyone wants clear results." Test out a slower or faster pace to see how that changes the flow.

Reflection Exercise

Grab a notebook or your notes app. After a call or meeting, jot down three word choices or patterns you heard. Script how you could have used one—in your style—in a reply. For the pacing part, note where you matched tempo well or where things felt awkward. Imagine, if you'd slowed down with that soft-spoken client, how might the rest of the conversation have opened up?

Some days, the right word lands at just the right time. But sometimes, the most powerful thing you can do is let a bit of silence ride out after a thoughtful phrase or pause on your reply to match the other person's pacing (Hoek et al., 2025).

Silence, the Student Mindset, and Learning

Think back to the first time you experimented with verbal mirroring—matching your client's language, tone, or even choice of words. You probably noticed how quickly rapport formed, how conversation seemed to "click" in ways it never had before. With comfort in mirroring, a new world opens up that's all about what isn't said. Silence becomes one of your strongest tools.

The Power of Strategic Silence

It takes courage to pause after you echo a client's priorities, or to leave a question hanging just long enough for them to dig a little deeper, but it's often in these moments that the conversation reveals the most.

Picture a sales conversation where you ask, "What worries you most about switching providers?" Instead of jumping in with your solution, you just wait. At first, it might feel tense. The client might shift in their chair, glance away, or hesitate. Eventually, though, the silence invites them to fill the space: "Honestly, it's not even about your product. I've had bad experiences with change before, and I don't want to go through that stress again." If you'd filled the gap with more talk, you might have missed the real story—the emotional obstacle standing between you and a deal.

This reminds me of what I learned as a 17-year-old behind that perfume counter, which I shared in Chapter 2. Sometimes, a customer would approach, visibly upset about something—maybe they'd had a terrible day, maybe they were frustrated with a previous purchase. My instinct was to talk, to fill the uncomfortable silence, to smooth things over with words. But I discovered that turning people's anger into empathy often meant shutting up first. Letting them vent. Giving them space. Recognizing their emotional cues in real time meant not just seeing their frustration but allowing room for it to dissipate naturally. That's when human connection as a sales tool really took hold.

Relying on silence requires the same presence as active listening. It means shutting down distractions and paying close attention not just to words but to nonverbal cues: the quick glance, a subtle sigh, the tightening of hands. When you wait after a mirrored statement, you signal genuine curiosity and allow your counterpart space to be honest. Pausing can feel risky; it runs against the grain of filling the air with clever lines or canned pitches. Yet, the psychological effect is powerful: most people feel compelled to end silence by elaborating or revealing a more profound truth (Cuncic, 2024).

Many seasoned professionals call this a "golden silence," the brief, unspoken interval after a tough question or a big reveal, where emotions settle and clarity rises. By staying silent in strategic places, you communicate attentiveness and respect; it's a gesture of trust, a way to tell the other person that their words matter enough to let them echo rather than rush them. Try this after your next mirrored phrase. Count silently to three and watch what emerges.

The Student Mindset

Shifting over to the power of the student mindset, think about walking into a new office where you know nobody and everything—software, jargon, unspoken rules—feels new. The instinct might be to perform, to act as if you've already mastered it all. But people who thrive in sales don't just perform; they learn at every turn. The "student mindset" means seeing every call and meeting as a lesson. Instead of fearing what you don't know or dreading mistakes, you stay curious (Cuncic, 2024).

I'll be honest: Even after years in this field, I still approach every significant conversation as a learning opportunity. The moment I think I've figured it all out is the moment I start missing the signals that matter most. That grieving woman with the $2,500 purchase, as I described in Chapter 4? She taught me something profound about how spotting nostalgia, grief, and surprise can completely transform a sales interaction. Every customer since has been another teacher.

Sales pros who succeed over the long haul never outgrow this approach. They see everyone around them as a potential source for learning, regardless of title or years in the field. Consider the top rep who starts her morning by scanning yesterday's call summaries, noting objections and what moved the conversation forward. She keeps a tiny notebook in her pocket—on one side, she writes "Wins" (closed deals, moments of breakthrough) and on the other, "Losses" (calls that faltered and why). She finishes the day by swapping stories with a peer, role-playing tricky conversations, and soliciting raw, honest feedback.

Wrapping It Up

Now that you've learned to tune into the subtle signals of body language, micro-expressions, and energy in sales conversations, you're ready to take your emotional intelligence to the next level. By paying attention to these clues—noticing the slight shifts in posture, facial flickers, and speech rhythm—you can build genuine rapport and adjust your approach in real time.

This isn't about tricks or pressure; it's about having real, human connections that make both you and your client feel seen and understood. I learned this lesson early, standing behind a perfume counter as a teenager, watching faces and reading rooms before I had any formal training. The skills I've shared in this chapter—from recognizing defensive signals to mastering strategic silence—all flow from that same fundamental insight: sales is ultimately about one human being truly seeing another.

As you practice matching energy, mirroring words, and embracing silence, you'll find that sales become less about pushing a product and more about creating trust. Keep experimenting with these skills. You're setting the stage for conversations that flow naturally and open doors to deeper, more meaningful outcomes in every deal.

Chapter 8:
You Are What You Believe and Show

Picture yourself scrolling through a playlist, trying to find the right song for your mood. Some tracks grab you within the first few seconds—no lyrics yet, just the tone, the rhythm, the energy. You lean in, curious, engaged, ready to hear more. Other songs, even if beautifully written, don't immediately spark that connection. You skip them, not because they're bad, but because something in those opening notes didn't resonate with you.

People work the same way. Long before we share our ideas, our presence plays its first few "notes." Our body language, energy, and sense of certainty create an impression—one that invites others to tune in or tune out. It's not about talent alone; it's about the signals we broadcast, often without realizing it.

This chapter is about learning to conduct that opening moment with intention. It's about understanding how your inner beliefs shape the "sound" you project—and how aligning the two can change the opportunities that come your way. When you show up as someone who believes deeply in their own worth, others start hearing you differently, too.

The Power of Showing Up: Why Your Daily Actions Matter More Than Your Résumé

Let's be honest: Confidence isn't some lucky trait you're born with. It's not about having the right parents or going to the right school. It's built through small, unglamorous actions that you repeat until they become who you are. Every single choice you make sends a signal to the people around you, whether you realize it or not. They notice when you show up—and how you show up. That's what determines whether they see you as someone they can count on.

Here's what most people miss: Leadership and credibility don't start when you're officially given a title or when you lead your first big meeting. They begin much earlier, in the quiet moments when nobody's watching. They're built through consistency.

I learned this lesson during my early days as a struggling teenage salesman, which I described in earlier chapters. I remember standing in a room full of experienced salespeople, feeling completely out of place. Most of them had years on me. They had suits that fit properly. They had client lists and closing techniques I'd never heard of. And there I was—a kid who barely looked old enough to drive, let alone sell anything to anyone.

But something shifted in me during one of those early meetings. I looked around at the veteran salespeople, some of whom were already checking their watches, already mentally planning their lunch breaks, already coasting on past wins. And I made a decision that would change everything. I said to myself, quietly but with absolute conviction: "I'm going to outlast all of you."

That single declaration reshaped my identity. It wasn't arrogance; it was a commitment. I decided in that moment that I wasn't just some kid trying to make a few bucks. I was going to become a sales warrior. Someone who treated this craft with the seriousness and dedication of a martial artist training for a championship fight.

Think about two people arriving for a morning meeting. The first person rushes in right as the clock strikes nine. They're already flustered, digging through their bag for their phone, looking slightly disheveled. The second person arrives five minutes early. Their bag is organized, their shoes are clean, and they're calm. They sit down, quickly review their notes, and greet the others with genuine warmth.

Before either person has said anything of substance, a message has already been sent. The second person is telling everyone: *I'm prepared. I'm present. I take this seriously.* And here's the remarkable part: People pick up on these signals almost automatically, the way you can feel a storm coming before the first drop of rain falls.

The Hidden Cost of Cutting Corners

Now, consider someone who regularly says they'll follow up or send that email—but doesn't. They promise a client an update by Friday, but Monday rolls around, and all anyone gets is a vague, apologetic message. Each time this happens, it's like a tiny withdrawal from their credibility bank account.

People remember these patterns. Maybe not consciously at first, but over time, they add up. Trust isn't built through grand gestures or one amazing performance. It's built through showing up consistently, keeping your promises, and following through on the small stuff.

During my early sales career, I watched colleagues cut corners constantly. They'd skip the follow-up calls. They'd show up late to client meetings. They'd half-prepare their presentations. And then they'd wonder why their numbers stayed flat while mine kept climbing.

The difference wasn't talent. The difference was that I had chosen hunger over comfort. As I mentioned in an earlier chapter, there was a period when I was surviving on $50 a week. Fifty dollars. That's not a typo. While other young people my age were spending money on entertainment and convenience, I was rationing every cent, investing everything back into my development and my craft.

That $50-a-week period taught me something invaluable: When you're hungry—really hungry—you don't have the luxury of cutting corners. Every opportunity matters. Every client interaction could be the one that changes your trajectory. You show up prepared because you can't afford *not* to.

Why Your Private Habits Shape Your Public Image

Here's something that might surprise you: Credibility is something people observe and measure, not something you can simply claim. Your actions speak louder than any LinkedIn summary or polished elevator pitch ever could. And people are watching—even in the routine moments you think don't matter.

Simple acts matter enormously. Keeping a promise. Arriving prepared. Checking in on a commitment without being asked. These micro-habits create ripple effects that shape how you're perceived across every relationship—whether it's with your boss, a potential client, or even yourself.

No bullet point on a résumé can compete with the power of always doing what you say you'll do, even when no one's explicitly watching.

I remember the exact moment I decided to shift my self-image from "kid" to "professional." I was preparing for a meeting with a prospect who was easily 30 years older than me. The night before, I laid out my clothes carefully. I polished my shoes until they reflected light. I reviewed my presentation so many times that I could recite it in my sleep.

When I walked into that meeting, something was different. The prospect looked at me—really looked at me—and I could see the moment his assessment shifted. He wasn't seeing a teenager anymore. He was seeing someone who took this seriously. Someone who had prepared. Someone worth listening to.

The Rituals That Reinforce Who You Are

Small, disciplined rituals often matter more than any single big performance. These aren't just habits; they're signals you're sending to your own brain about your identity.

Setting up your workspace before diving into work tells your mind, "This matters. I'm a professional." Taking time to lay out your clothes the night before or keeping your shoes polished isn't superficial vanity; it's a cue about who you believe you are. Practicing a pitch in front of a mirror goes deeper than hope or positive thinking. When you act like you belong before anyone tells you that you do, confidence begins to align with reality, not wishful fantasy.

This is where your inner belief and outer presence start to match. Someone who clears the clutter from their desk before opening their laptop, or who reviews tomorrow's priorities the night before, is actively practicing reliability. They're training themselves to be the person they want to become.

I developed my own rituals during those lean years. Every morning, before I made a single call, I would stand in front of the mirror and remind myself who I was becoming. Not who I was—who I was becoming. A sales warrior. Someone who saw this not as a temporary job but as a lifelong craft worth mastering.

Leading Through Presence, Not Proclamation

Real presence doesn't come from talking about leadership—it comes from embodying it in small, everyday ways. People mirror what they see. They pick up on your energy, your mood, your level of readiness, often before you've said a word.

When you show up with quiet assurance—even in small ways—you give others permission to feel secure and steady too. But if you're rushing, cutting corners, or making excuses, the people around you will unconsciously pick up on that, too. Self-discipline doesn't just build your confidence; it creates a ripple effect in your environment. People look for these cues to guide their own behavior and expectations.

One of the most critical mindset shifts I made was learning to embrace pressure and challenge rather than avoid them. Most people run from difficult situations. They avoid the tough prospects, the complicated objections, the high-stakes presentations. I learned to run toward them.

Every challenging situation became an opportunity to prove—to myself and to others—that I belonged. When a prospect raised a difficult objection, I didn't crumble. I leaned in. When a deal fell through at the last minute, I didn't sulk. I analyzed what went wrong and prepared to do better next time.

Your Daily Professionalism Ritual

Want to start reinforcing your professional self-image today? Try these three simple actions:

1. Set tomorrow's priorities tonight. Before you finish your day, write down your three biggest priorities for tomorrow. This way, you won't spend your morning reacting—you'll start with intention.

2. Do one small grooming task. Take a minute to polish your shoes, trim your nails, or do one small piece of personal grooming. You're sending a signal to yourself that details count.

3. Visualize arriving early. Look at your calendar and mentally plan to arrive five minutes early to each appointment. Picture yourself walking into the room calm, ready, and open.

Imagine someone standing in front of the mirror, practicing their presentation out loud. They're not just rehearsing words; they're watching their own body language, reading their energy, learning to project the confidence they want others to see. Another person clears their desk before logging in for the day, checking their calendar to avoid surprises, and greeting the morning with quiet purpose.

Each choice is small on its own. But together, they form a pattern that teaches others what to expect—and, just as importantly, trains you to see a capable, credible person every time you look in the mirror.

The Invisible Transfer: How Your Energy Shapes Every Interaction

Understanding Emotional Contagion

Here's something most people don't realize: Everyone around you is constantly picking up on invisible signals you're sending, often before you've said a single word. Walk into a room with confidence—relaxed posture, a spark in your eyes, steady breathing—and even the most distracted person will pause and notice. But shift into uncertainty, let your shoulders slump or your voice waver, and watch how quickly attention slips away.

This phenomenon is called emotional contagion, and it's incredibly powerful. Research shows that our brains are hardwired to pick up cues from the people around us, matching their mood, enthusiasm, and energy almost instantly (Petitta et al., 2021). The energy you bring into a conversation, meeting, or even a casual interaction becomes the baseline for everyone else in the room.

The Store Example: Energy in Action

Think about walking into a retail store. You're greeted by an employee who looks bored and listless, eyes darting to the clock. Within seconds, your own interest dulls. Maybe you decide that whatever you came for can wait another day.

Now, imagine a different scenario: a salesperson stands tall, makes genuine eye contact, and offers a warm, steady smile. You feel pulled in, engaged, even before you've decided whether you're ready to buy anything.

This isn't random. It's a predictable response. When someone's body language and tone signal confidence and warmth, the people around them unconsciously begin to mirror it. Even subtle things make a difference: a calm voice, open hands instead of crossed arms, a steady rhythm instead of rushed speech. All these cues register in people's brains before their conscious thinking catches up.

The Science Behind the Feeling

Research shows that emotions spread quickly through groups—almost like a cold moving through an office. If one person in a team or social setting displays a certain emotional state, those nearby begin to synchronize—sometimes moving together toward optimism and energy, other times toward anxiety and doubt (Hazy & Boyatzis, 2015).

Even silent cues matter enormously. How quickly you move. The way you settle into a chair. These details give away more than most people realize. Emotional contagion doesn't ask for permission—it just happens. In every sales call or negotiation, the emotional tone you set might be driving the other person's gut feeling about whether they trust you, long before you finish your first sentence.

I discovered this truth during my early selling days when I noticed something puzzling: My results varied dramatically depending on my mood when I walked in the door. On days when I felt defeated before I even started, prospects seemed to pick up on that energy immediately. But on days when I walked in feeling like the sales warrior I was becoming, something shifted in how people responded to me.

Your Pre-Interaction Energy Reset

Self-awareness becomes your first real tool. You can't change what you don't notice. Is your tone clipped because you're tired? Are you nervously fidgeting without realizing it? The smallest lapses can break the emotional contract you're trying to establish.

But here's the good news: You can train yourself to notice, reset, and intentionally lead the emotional tempo. Try this simple pre-interaction ritual:

1. Set a timer for 30 seconds before any important interaction— whether it's a meeting, call, or sales pitch. Stand up. Roll your shoulders back. Take three deep breaths. Plant your feet flat on the ground.

2. Ask yourself out loud: "Am I giving off the kind of energy I'd want to buy from?"

3. Notice what you find. Sagging posture? Flat tone? Racing mind? If you notice any of these, make an adjustment: Lift your chest, put a half-smile on your face, lower your shoulders.

4. Imagine the other person matching your current energy. If that wouldn't get you the results you want, use your breath and body to deliberately raise your energy.

5. Only begin the conversation when you intentionally feel yourself transmitting the vibe you want to receive in return.

This isn't about faking it. It's about consciously managing the silent conversation that shapes trust and belief in you before you've even started talking. When you do this consistently, you'll notice responses improve, conversations feel easier, and people remember you for your presence—not just your words.

First Impressions: Why What You Wear Speaks Before You Do

The Seven-Second Window

From the moment you walk into any room—a sales meeting, networking event, or job interview—what you wear, how you're groomed, and even your posture start shaping opinions before you've opened your mouth. That "emotional charge" people pick up when you enter? It's amplified by your outward presence.

Research has shown that first impressions form in about seven seconds. Seven seconds. That's how long you have before people make firm conclusions about whether you're competent, reliable, or worth listening to (Gibbons, 2018).

Imagine arriving at a high-stakes client meeting after a rushed morning. Your blazer's wrinkled. Your hair is falling in your eyes. Your shoes have visible scuff marks. Even though you've prepared an excellent pitch, something feels off. And when your appearance shows that lack of intention, the client's first impression is colored by it—affecting their willingness to trust your expertise before you've said anything substantial.

The Subconscious Shortcut

Psychologists call this snap judgment a "subconscious shortcut." Our brains are wired to quickly size up credibility and trustworthiness based on visual cues. And here's what's interesting: This isn't about expensive labels or trendy fashion. The cues that matter most are fit, tidiness, grooming, posture, and subtle details like fresh breath or clean nails.

Every element of your appearance becomes a silent messenger. Neat, well-chosen clothes that fit properly say you respect the opportunity and yourself. Clean hair, fresh breath, and upright posture transmit capability and readiness. When details are off—chipped nail polish, a wrinkled collar, overpowering cologne—people unconsciously start doubting your attention to detail in other areas too.

During my $50-a-week period, I couldn't afford expensive clothes. But I could afford to keep what I had impeccably clean and pressed. I could afford to polish my shoes until they gleamed. I could afford to stand up straight and look people in the eye.

The Two-Way Mirror of Appearance

The way you present yourself acts like your reputation's advance guard, quietly shaping whether you'll be viewed as trustworthy or overlooked. But this isn't only about external judgment. It goes deeper—it actually changes the way you see and feel about yourself.

There's a concept called "enclothed cognition" that explains this phenomenon: The clothes you wear don't just shape how others see you—they affect your own confidence, focus, and mood (Robinson, 2025). When you wear something that fits well and makes you feel strong, it can cause subtle yet real shifts in how you carry yourself.

A sharp blazer or a perfectly paired outfit is more than fabric; it's emotional armor you slip into before facing a big day. Even small changes, like upgrading from sneakers to polished shoes or choosing a style that reflects your personality, can make every challenge feel more manageable.

Practical Steps for Aligning Your Look With Your Goals

Getting this right doesn't have to be overwhelming. Pay attention to context. What's expected in your industry? Are you selling enterprise software? Aim for clean lines, neutral tones, and classic fits. Working in a creative field? You have more freedom to introduce color, bold accessories, or trend-forward pieces—but keep it intentional and coordinated.

Match the room while highlighting your uniqueness. The goal is to fit the environment's tone while still showing who you are. Authenticity beats imitation every time. Don't force yourself into styles that feel like a costume. Look at leaders you admire, then adapt their approach in a way that feels natural to you.

Your Grooming and Credibility Checklist

Here are the details that quietly signal you care—about your work, your relationships, and your standards: upright posture with relaxed shoulders, a confident handshake that's firm but not crushing, clean and trimmed nails, fresh breath especially after coffee or before meetings, a subtle and clean scent, tidy hair styled to look intentional, clean and fitted clothes without stains or wrinkles, and polished shoes that coordinate with your outfit.

When these elements align, you create what becomes your daily "personal brand." Over time, this consistency becomes a silent reputation. Think about a manager whose appearance consistently telegraphs confidence and reliability—clients and team members learn to expect high standards. Compare that to someone who sometimes looks sharp and sometimes doesn't. The result is confusion, and trust builds much more slowly.

The Inner Game: Mental Techniques That Turn Belief Into Reality

The Power of Acting "As If"

Picture a salesperson standing in front of the mirror before heading to work. He's feeling anxious, worried that today's prospects might see right through him. But then he makes one simple mental shift: he tells himself, "I believe in this product. I know it makes a difference." He repeats it until something changes—his posture straightens, his breathing steadies.

At his next meeting, instead of nervously reciting his rehearsed pitch, he speaks with genuine conviction. For the first time in weeks, a tough client actually leans forward, intrigued and engaged. That single moment—daring to act as if he belonged—kicks off a series of wins that multiplies his confidence and fundamentally changes how people respond to him.

I lived this transformation. When I declared "I'm going to outlast all of you," I wasn't making a prediction based on evidence. I was making a decision about my identity. I was choosing to act as if I were already the sales warrior I wanted to become—even though I had no proof yet that I could actually become that person.

The Belief-Action-Proof Cycle

This is the cycle at the heart of true confidence: belief-action-proof-belief. You act in faith before you fully feel it. Then, one real-world success turns that action into tangible proof, which reinforces your belief. It's not about faking it or putting on a show. It's about rehearsing your potential until small results give your mind the evidence it needs.

This is exactly how athletes prepare. They script victory in their minds long before any competition begins—because imagination prepares both body and mind for what's coming (Corona, 2025).

The beautiful thing about this cycle is that it builds momentum. Each small win creates evidence that your belief is justified. That evidence makes the next bold action easier. Which creates more evidence. Which makes the next action easier still.

During my early career, I deliberately sought out situations that would create proof for my developing identity. I volunteered for the difficult presentations. I asked for the challenging prospects. I put myself in positions where success would be meaningful—not because I was certain I would succeed, but because I knew that even the attempt would reshape my self-image.

Visualization: Your Morning Mental Rehearsal

Visualizing success each day strengthens this belief muscle. Here's a practical guide anyone can use:

1. Find a quiet space before your day starts—maybe while your coffee brews or right after you wake up.

2. Close your eyes and picture a specific win. It could be a client handshake after closing a deal, applause after a presentation, or hearing the confident tone in your own voice during a meeting. Make it as vivid as possible. What do you see? What do you hear? What do you feel?

3. Hold this mental scene for at least 60 seconds. Let the details become real in your mind's eye—the lighting in the room, the expressions on faces, the feeling of accomplishment in your chest.

4. Open your eyes and carry that imagined victory with you as you move into your day.

Why does this work? Because your brain doesn't easily distinguish between vividly imagined events and actual memories. Visual images send signals through the same neural circuits you'll activate when you perform for real. If you dread making presentations, take a private moment beforehand to envision yourself at the conference table, relaxed and articulate. When things feel shaky mid-presentation, mentally return to that image and borrow its certainty for just long enough to steady your voice and hands.

Affirmations That Actually Work

Daily affirmations offer a second, science-backed tool for upgrading self-belief. But here's the catch: They only work if you actually believe them. Choose statements that feel authentic and keep them focused. If you're in a credibility-driven field, try phrases like: "I sell with purpose and integrity," "My confidence earns trust," or "Every conversation brings me closer to success."

Repeat them out loud each morning and just before high-pressure moments—right before a pitch, or as you're walking into a first client call. The value isn't in empty positive thinking. It's in carving a new groove in your brain's default playlist.

Affirmations replace old patterns of self-doubt with repeated, believable reminders of what you're capable of. This practice reshapes your neural pathways through something called "cognitive restructuring," training your mind to play a new tape until positive messages feel as real as past criticism once did (*Affirmations - Anxiety Skill Building*, 2025).

My personal affirmation during those early years was simple: "I am a sales warrior mastering a lifelong craft." I repeated it every morning. I repeated it before difficult calls. I repeated it after rejections. And slowly, imperceptibly, it stopped feeling like something I was trying to become and started feeling like something I simply was.

Anchoring: Your Instant Confidence Switch

Anchoring gives you a third powerful tool for triggering confidence on command. Before your next important meeting, choose a specific gesture—a deliberate deep breath, touching a favorite watch or piece of jewelry, or adjusting your collar. Each time you recall a previous success or a powerful personal quality, perform this gesture. As you repeat this pairing over time, your brain begins linking the physical movement with the confident feeling.

Eventually, the gesture itself triggers a small surge of presence and assurance. It works the same way certain songs can instantly transport you back to treasured memories.

Use these strategies as active rehearsal, not passive wishful thinking. They turn forced effort into natural ability over time. The magic happens not through magic at all—it happens through daily, deliberate action.

Confidence becomes a habit, not a mask. You practice acting bold, trustworthy, and solid. Small rewards show your subconscious mind what you're truly capable of. And gradually, what once required effort becomes simply who you are (*Affirmations - Anxiety Skill Building*, 2025).

Sustaining Confidence: Building a Foundation That Lasts

The Authenticity Advantage

You've learned powerful mental techniques—visualization, affirmations, anchoring. These tools work. But here's what makes them sustainable: grounding them in authenticity. Confidence that lasts doesn't come from acting a part. It comes from building daily habits and environments that genuinely reinforce who you're becoming.

When you show up authentically—not pretending to be someone you're not—your brain rewards you with genuine self-assurance. And the people around you? They pick up on that real conviction (Moore, 2025).

Genuine confidence has its roots in honest self-presentation. Imagine a team leader faced with a tough question in front of their group. The leader who says, "I don't have that answer right now, but I'll find it and get back to you," creates immediate trust. The team knows their leader has their interests at heart and believes in finding real solutions.

Compare that to someone who dodges the question or tries to fake their way through an answer. That forced facade falls apart quickly, leaving people wondering what else might not be quite true. Authentic presence shows through calm eye contact, admitting limits without apologizing, and maintaining steady body language. People instinctively sense whether your confidence comes from genuine belief or nervous bluffing.

Your Environment Shapes Your Confidence

The spaces where you live and work have a bigger impact on your confidence than most people realize. Trying to work at a kitchen table piled high with bills, laundry, and yesterday's dishes sends subtle signals of chaos to your brain. It's distracting and deflating.

Now, picture that same person at a small but clean desk with a quality notebook, a favorite pen, good lighting, and a charged phone within reach. Suddenly, the whole mood shifts. These minor upgrades might seem trivial, but they set powerful mental expectations. You're signaling to yourself—and eventually to everyone else—that you're someone who pays attention to detail and expects good things from your work.

Small Rituals, Big Impact

Daily rituals quietly reinforce this professional mindset. Shining your shoes, straightening your appearance, or carefully reviewing the day's plan isn't about vanity. These actions send a clear message: "I am disciplined. I care about how I show up. I am prepared."

Laying out your outfit the night before eliminates morning decision fatigue and gives you a sense of readiness from the moment you wake up. Going over your affirmations while you get dressed sharpens your focus for the day ahead. These smart routines, repeated consistently, shape not only how you see yourself but how your entire day unfolds (Moore, 2025).

Your Victory File: Proof for Tough Days

Difficult times come for everyone. They can threaten even the strongest self-image. This is when having concrete proof of your abilities becomes crucial.

Create a "Victory File"—either a folder on your computer or a physical folder in a drawer. Fill it with positive feedback, thank-you notes, certificates, screenshots of great reviews, or emails of recognition. When your confidence dips, take a few minutes to review these memories. They bring back moments where your ability clearly shone.

Add to this by staying connected with positive peers, friends, or colleagues who help you keep setbacks in perspective. Remind yourself, "I'm gathering experience for my future wins." This mindset keeps you steady in the face of mistakes or temporary failures ("Confidence vs Arrogance," 2025).

Wrapping It Up

When I declared, "I'm going to outlast all of you," I wasn't predicting the future. I was creating it. When I chose hunger over comfort, I wasn't suffering—I was investing. When I shifted my self-image from "kid" to "professional," I wasn't pretending—I was claiming an identity that my actions would eventually justify.

Sales became more than a job for me. It became a lifelong craft— something worthy of the same dedication and discipline that masters bring to any art form. And the pressure and challenges that drove others away? They became the very things that forged my confidence into something unshakeable.

You're ready to take control of how others see you. More importantly, you're prepared to take control of how you see yourself. The choice is yours. Start small. Start today. And watch what happens when you become the person you've been visualizing all along.

Chapter 9:
Setting Sales Goals

Have you ever set a sales goal only to find it slipping further away as the days go by? Wonder why some goals feel motivating while others just hang over your head like a heavy cloud? What if there was a way to turn those big, overwhelming targets into clear steps you can actually take each day?

Setting sales goals isn't just about picking a number and hoping for the best. It's about creating goals that challenge you without crushing you, guiding your daily actions, and helping you learn from every win or miss. This chapter digs into how to build goals that are specific, measurable, and rooted in purpose. You'll see how breaking down annual dreams into simple daily tasks turns what feels impossible into something doable—and even exciting.

We'll also explore how to maintain your motivation, leverage accountability to your advantage, and turn setbacks into valuable lessons that push you forward. By the end, you'll have a clear path to set goals that don't just look good on paper but truly move the needle every single day.

SMART Goals: Specific and Measurable

Numbers only matter if they point you to goals you can actually hit. Achievable goals spark growth without pushing you into fight-or-flight mode. When your goal is too easy, you start phoning it in. There's no challenge to wake you up in the morning, so you settle for safe results. But crank that dial too far and you get the opposite problem: "I should do fifty deals this month," when your historic best is eight. Stress builds, you fudge your numbers, or avoid the whole target entirely.

I learned this lesson the hard way during my early sales career. As I mentioned in earlier chapters, I went through a dramatic pay transition—from making $250 a week down to just $50 a week. That wasn't a typo or a temporary dip. That was my reality, week after week.

That pay cut could have destroyed me. Most people in that situation would have quit, found something more stable, something that guaranteed a paycheck. But I saw it differently. That $50 a week wasn't failure; it was fuel. It was the clearest motivation I'd ever had. Every single dollar I wanted to earn beyond that pittance would come purely from commission. There was no safety net, no base salary to fall back on, no cushion to make me comfortable.

That commission hunger created a focus I'd never experienced before. When you're living on $50 a week, every prospect matters. Every call matters. Every follow-up could be the difference between eating well or scraping by. There's no room for laziness, no space for excuses, no option to coast.

The Sweet Spot: Stretch But Don't Snap

"Stretch but don't snap" means you want a goal that feels like a test, something that makes you ask, "Can I really do that if I give my best?" Take a rep used to closing five deals each month at a 20% conversion rate. The best version of them might push to close seven a month with a slightly better close rate or a bit more prospecting. Doubling or tripling it overnight would be fiction, not a stretch.

When you set your target, ask, "Is this what the best version of me can hit if I push, learn, and adapt each day?" Stack the facts: Review your current sales cycle, ask which parts are controllable, and be honest about what growth looks like one step beyond what feels safe.

During my $50-a-week period, I couldn't afford fantasy goals. I needed goals that were ambitious but grounded in reality. So, I built my targets around one simple, powerful idea: building a customer base intentionally.

I decided I would accumulate 50 to 70 customers—not all at once, but systematically, one at a time. Each new customer represented not just a single sale but a potential stream of repeat business. I wasn't just chasing commissions; I was building an asset that would compound over time.

Making Goals Relevant

Another trap in sales goal setting is chasing numbers for numbers' sake. Relevance answers the question, "Will hitting this actually help me build the career or business I want?" If you push high-volume, low-margin deals just to boost your closes, but the commissions barely move your income or these clients churn fast, you burn out fast.

Relevant goals are the ones that connect daily action to long-term momentum. For sales pros, that means prioritizing high-quality client relationships, targeting accounts that value your expertise, and building recurring business streams. The goal to "increase average client contract value by 15% by deepening relationships with three core accounts each quarter" might mean fewer transactions, but it strengthens your bottom line and builds a network that pays off for years (Bloomenthal, 2024).

I understood something that many salespeople miss: acquisition is expensive, but retention is profitable. So, I developed what I called my 80% retention strategy. My goal wasn't just to get customers—it was to keep 80% or more of them coming back, month after month, year after year.

This changed everything about how I approached sales. Every interaction became an opportunity to build trust, not just close a deal. Every promise I made, I kept. Every follow-up mattered. Because I knew that losing a customer meant starting from scratch, and I couldn't afford that—not financially, and not strategically.

When you're living on $50 a week, you learn fast that it's far easier to sell to someone who already trusts you than to constantly chase new prospects. Those 50 to 70 customers became my foundation. They were the difference between survival and success.

The Power of Deadlines

Deadlines change everything. If you write down a goal but don't add "by when," your brain stores it as someday territory, where dreams go to die. Set a date and the goal steps into the present, with real stakes (*The Power of Putting Pen to Paper*, 2024). Think of "I'll prospect more" vs. "I'll make 20 calls by 3 p.m. every Tuesday and Thursday." The second one tells your calendar, your brain, and anyone watching when you'll either win or miss.

To keep urgency high but manageable, break big goals into chunks across time: a year's target becomes a monthly marker, which feeds a weekly target, and then a daily minimum. Each checkpoint gives you a chance to reflect, realign, or double down on effort without letting the weeks slip by unnoticed.

Breaking Down the Annual Goal

Let's put the framework into action with the classic $1 million sales goal:

1. **Divide $1 million by 12 months:** That's $83,000 per month. If the average deal is $10,000, you need roughly 8 or 9 deals monthly.

2. **Assume a 25% close rate:** Now, you need 36 qualified opportunities to net those deals. If you land one qualified lead for every 10 prospecting calls, you're looking at 360 calls a month—about 18 a working day.

These numbers aren't fantasy; they're built from your real-world inputs. Working backwards transforms the mountain ahead into a series of steps beneath your feet.

Daily Metrics Drive Action

Annual goals often paralyze, but daily metrics mobilize. Looking up at $1 million can send you back under the covers. Seeing "make 18 calls today" feels doable; it's a task, not a wish. Daily numbers guide your habits, and habits build momentum. Day by day, calls turn into conversations, conversations grow into opportunities, and the year's goal shifts from intimidating to routine.

This is where daily consistency becomes your superpower. During my early career, I created non-negotiable daily standards for myself. No matter how I felt, no matter what happened the day before, I had a minimum number of activities I would complete every single day.

Some days, I felt unstoppable. Other days, I wanted to quit. But the daily standard didn't care about my feelings. It was the anchor that kept me moving forward when motivation failed. And here's what I discovered: Daily consistency doesn't just produce short-term results. It creates long-term transformation.

Those 50 to 70 customers I built? They didn't appear overnight. They accumulated through daily action, one conversation at a time, one relationship at a time. Each day I showed up and did the work, even when I didn't see immediate results. Especially when I didn't see immediate results.

The Power of Micro-Goals

Micro-goals keep your engine running on the rough days. When "build my pipeline" sounds too big, shrink it: "send three LinkedIn connection requests before noon." That win signals progress and dials down procrastination. Micro-goals help with follow-ups ("Email two clients for check-ins before 10 a.m."), deepening relationships ("Share an article with one prospect each morning"), and growing your skills ("Read one case study weekly"). Every small act builds confidence and keeps you engaged, turning progress into a daily reward.

My micro-goals during the $50-a-week period were ruthlessly practical. Call five prospects before lunch. Send three follow-up messages before the end of the day. Connect with one existing customer to check in on their needs. These weren't glamorous activities. But they were the building blocks of the customer base that would eventually lift me out of poverty.

Your Sales Dashboard

A sales dashboard anchors accountability. Track metrics like daily calls, new meetings, proposals out, wins, and revenue earned. Whether you use a whiteboard, a Google Sheet with your team, or an app like HubSpot, seeing numbers tick upward is a boost no pep talk can match.

I tracked everything. Not because I was obsessive, but because I needed to see proof that my effort was creating momentum. On hard days—and there were many—I could look at my dashboard and see that my customer base was growing, that my retention rate was holding, that my daily actions were adding up to something real.

Staying Motivated and Using Accountability

When you see sales numbers appear on your dashboard each day, the logic seems simple: just follow the path, hit your metrics, and the goals will take care of themselves. Real life has a few more twists. Even with perfect math and tracking, each new win or loss sends you on an emotional rollercoaster that messes with your routine. Sales brings out the highs of a killer month and the lows of a dry spell—sometimes in the very same week. Left unchecked, those swings can wreck your best-laid plans. That's where discipline and a few steady habits step in.

Handling Success

After a stretch of success, it's tempting to take your foot off the gas. Closing a huge deal or crushing your weekly quota feels like permission to coast, but that's when discipline matters most. You want to spend a moment celebrating—the win is real, and you earned it. Give yourself a dinner out or a shout-out on your team chat. Then, ask yourself what actions led to that win. Was it a bold follow-up email, a killer product demo, or three coffee meetings you booked the week before?

Break down exactly what paid off, write it down, and look for patterns. Consistency trumps luck in sales. If you know what works, try to repeat those same behaviors every single week. Set a daily action goal that lines up with your metrics, like making 20 calls or booking five meetings, no matter how good last month was.

I learned early on that success could be more dangerous than failure if I let it make me complacent. Every time I landed a new customer, there was a temptation to relax, to think I'd "made it." But I knew that my 80% retention strategy only worked if I kept serving those customers with the same intensity I used to win them in the first place.

Handling Setbacks

Handling a bad week takes a different kind of discipline. It's easy to let frustration take over and start second-guessing your talent. One off month or a string of rejections does not make you a bad salesperson. Your numbers show performance, not identity. If you feel discouraged, dig deeper: Did you actually put in the same effort? Was your pitch less sharp, or did you try a new outreach method that flopped?

Instead of assigning blame, get curious. Every "no" hides a lesson. Maybe you left out a key question in discovery calls, or maybe you lost focus after two rejections in a row. Treat each letdown like feedback. Ask what tiny adjustment could raise your odds next time—a tighter intro, a stronger objection-handling story, or just sending that follow-up email you skipped. This mindset resets pressure into progress.

During my toughest weeks—when I was still making $50 and wondering if this would ever work—I had to develop goals that could survive hard weeks. Goals that didn't crumble the moment things went wrong.

The key was focusing on what I could control. I couldn't control whether a prospect said yes. I couldn't control market conditions or competition. But I could control my daily activities. I could control my attitude. I could control whether I showed up and did the work, even when results weren't immediately visible.

This is what separates professionals from amateurs. Amateurs quit when things get hard. Professionals understand that hard weeks are part of the process, not evidence that the process has failed.

The One Day Rule

To avoid letting emotions stick around too long, try the "One Day Rule." The idea is simple: Good or bad, you get exactly one day to feel everything fully, and then you start again. Treat yourself after a monster win, but show up the next day ready to work, not to replay the highlight reel. Nurse the sting after a missed deal, but put boundaries on the gloom by literally setting a reminder to get back to business in the morning.

When you hit a huge goal or tough setback, first name the feeling—celebration, disappointment, relief, whatever. Block time that evening or next morning to process: celebrate or vent, solo or with your team. Set a literal deadline. This could mean sleeping it off, journaling, or putting it in your shared Slack group. After the deadline, physically mark the reset—close a browser tab, cross the day off your planner, or write "new start" at the top of a fresh page. Start the new day by returning to your controllable daily metrics—calls, meetings, or whatever matters most.

The Power of Accountability Partners

While discipline handles your own emotional extremes, accountability keeps you honest when motivation fizzles. Telling yourself to do something lacks bite—declare your goal to someone, and there's instant weight. An accountability partner works because the fear of letting someone else down is stronger than the fear of disappointing yourself.

Think about who plays this role best. Maybe it's a coworker also chasing numbers, a manager who pushes your comfort zone, or a friend or spouse rooting for you to show up for what matters. Mentors bring honest feedback and real experience. Colleagues build friendly competition.

Pick your partner and agree on a check-in time each week. Prepare your numbers and habits ahead of time—"I hit my call target but missed two follow-ups." Celebrate each other's wins out loud. Analyze the misses together—ask, "What made it hard? Did I avoid tough calls or just get unlucky?" Instead of focusing only on final results, track daily actions.

A sales team can amplify this effect with public leaderboards, whiteboards covered with names and tallies, or shared dashboards. When everyone sees the numbers, you share the load and turn discipline from a lonely job into a group effort (*Reframe Your Setbacks*, 2024).

Recognizing and Reversing Burnout

Sales consistency often hinges on systems and accountability, but drive fades fast when internal struggles go unaddressed. Even those who once thrived under daily goals and team support can slide into exhaustion that simple willpower can't fix. Burnout isn't a failure of character. It's a temporary energy crisis—a misalignment between what's demanded and the resources left to give.

Early Warning Signs

Early signs of burnout can be subtle at first but grow sharper with time. Dreading calls or meetings becomes the morning norm, even on days with big opportunities. Rejection starts to feel personal, making setbacks sting far past the moment. Tracking performance drops off as metrics become reminders of what's not working. Wins don't excite; a new sale looks like another chore, not a triumph. Losing patience with clients or snapping at teammates. Emotional energy sags, and the craft begins to feel pointless.

Use these warning signs as a checklist. If you spot more than one, pause to assess, not criticize.

Root Causes

The roots of burnout rarely come down to lack of talent or laziness. Overwork without regular rest is the most common culprit—a day off becomes just another empty promise. Weak boundaries let work seep into every evening and weekend. Lacking a long-term purpose makes daily wins feel random and hollow. When hard work comes without strategic direction or clear next steps, even the best efforts fall flat (Noor, 2022).

Burnout Recovery Process

Recognize where you stand today by checking those early symptoms. Here's a simple, four-step process for pulling yourself back:

1. Implement micro-breaks. Set three alarms on your phone, spaced across the day. Each time the alarm dings, step away for five minutes. Walk the hall, stretch, breathe with your eyes closed, or simply look out a window. These breaks calm your nervous system and prevent stress from building up unchecked.

2. Schedule real recovery time. Waiting to "find" time for yourself never works. Block gym visits, reading hours, or family dinners directly onto your calendar—mark them as non-negotiable, like meetings with your most important client. Protect this space fiercely.

3. Write your personal why. In one sentence, pin down what selling makes possible for you or those you care about. Maybe it's providing security for your family or reaching your own potential. Keep your why visible—on your desk or home screen. Read it each morning to remind yourself of the purpose behind every call.

4. Practice detaching from results. After missed targets or failed deals, write: "This outcome reflects my current strategy and circumstances, not my potential or worth. What will I adjust next time?" This stops you from internalizing setbacks as final verdicts and instead frames them as solvable puzzles.

Reframing Missed Targets as Data

When a goal goes unmet, the sting is real, but there's no lasting value in judging yourself. Shift your mindset from failure to diagnosis. Missed targets become feedback—just data that points to the next right move. Did conversion rates slip compared to your usual? Were incoming leads lower quality than in past months? Did you make as many follow-up calls as you planned?

Each answer highlights an area for adjustment, not self-punishment. These are variables in a system, not evidence of flawed effort.

Tracking the process instead of just the outcome gives you leverage. Focus on actions that you control—calls made, prep time before meetings, consistency of follow-up—rather than the ultimate prospect decision. Suppose your target was ten new sales, but you finished with six. You investigate and notice a big drop in follow-ups. Rather than wondering about talent or luck, you see a clear gap—a fixable process error.

Momentum matters more than perfection. Missing once or twice makes little difference if you return to your productive routines. Progress means showing up and working the process, even after rough weeks (Noor, 2022).

Purpose, Vision, and Daily Discipline

Bouncing back from missed targets and burnout means more than simply getting back on track; it gives you a blank canvas to ask new questions about why you do this work. Once you've learned to see failure as data and refuse to let a bad day become a bad month, the real opportunity comes into focus: lining up your daily sales activity with a purpose that fuels you for the long haul.

Finding Your Deeper Why

Too many sales professionals get lost chasing numbers for numbers' sake. They set aggressive targets, push hard at the start, and then fade because there's no fire underneath the math. Chasing income or recognition only gets you so far—when headwinds hit, these surface-level motivations quickly lose their power. The real game changer is figuring out what those numbers actually mean for your life.

Ask yourself what truly matters underneath each number. Why do you want that bonus check? What would hitting that quota provide outside of status or a moment at the top of the leaderboard? Surface motivations like money or status provide a jolt but rarely stick. Deeper reasons—family security, personal growth, serving clients in a way that changes their lives, building a reputation that will outlast this year's leaderboards—create stability that survives adversity (*Developing Mission, Vision, and Values*, n.d.).

For me, during those $50-a-week days, my why was crystal clear: survival first, then freedom. I wanted to prove to myself that I could build something from nothing. I wanted to create security that didn't depend on someone else's paycheck. And I wanted to master a craft that would serve me for life.

That deeper why is what kept me going when the commission checks were small and the rejections were many. It's what made me protect my customer relationships like they were gold—because they were. Those 50 to 70 customers represented more than just revenue. They represented proof that my strategy was working, that daily consistency was paying off, that I was building something real.

Crafting Your Personal Vision Statement

A personal vision statement ties these deeper values into a simple, powerful sentence or paragraph that you can carry with you every day. Close your eyes and picture the ideal version of your sales career one year from now. Describe your daily routine using all your senses—how does your morning feel, what energy do you bring to each meeting, what feedback do you get from clients and colleagues?

Think about the person you're becoming through this process, not just what you're achieving. Consider who benefits from your work—the people at home, the clients who rely on you, the positive changes that ripple out from your effort. Write it all down.

Example: "I wake up excited to deliver value to clients, confident in what I offer, and committed to leaving every conversation better than I found it. Each day, I push beyond comfort so I can provide my family with options I never had, mentor my teammates, and become a trusted partner to those I serve."

This isn't just a motivational poster. It's an emotional compass. Each morning, read it aloud. Visualize yourself succeeding, handling tough calls with grace, and celebrating wins that matter to you. Every quarter, check in: Do your concrete goals still support this vision? (*Developing Mission, Vision, and Values*, n.d.).

Five Honest Questions

Moving from abstract dreams to action means turning inward and facing five honest questions. Write your answers, review them regularly, and let them guide your tweaks to daily routines:

- *What specific sales number excites me, and what will that number change in my life?*

- *What do I commit to do each day, rain or shine, that guarantees progress toward my goal?*

- *What obstacles have halted my progress before, and what is my plan for handling them next time?*

- *Who will I report my results to, and how will I ensure accountability stays real?*

- *Why does this goal matter so much—what story or value is at the very core of my drive?*

Daily Discipline Checklist

Review goals and metrics every morning. Make at least one uncomfortable call daily. Log results honestly. Share progress with your accountability partner. Visualize your long-term purpose before ending the day.

Structure brings clarity, but discipline gives you the muscle to build a real legacy. Strategy transforms scattered results into repeatable patterns. Each call, every goal tracked, each setback recorded and learned from—these are the bricks of the reputation you'll stand on years from now. Set stretch targets. Track progress as if your growth depends on it—because it does (*Developing Mission, Vision, and Values*, n.d.).

Wrapping It Up

Now that you've learned how to build clear, measurable sales goals that break big ambitions into daily actions, you're set up to turn uncertainty into momentum. I know this system works because I lived it. I went from $50 a week to building a customer base that changed my life— not through luck or talent alone, but through daily consistency and goals that survived hard weeks. Those 50 to 70 customers I intentionally built, combined with my 80% retention strategy, created a foundation that compounded over time.

The commission hunger that came from making almost nothing forced me to focus like I'd never focused before. Every day mattered. Every customer mattered. Every relationship was an investment in my future.

Remember, it's not just about hitting numbers but connecting those numbers to a purpose that fuels you day after day. With this framework in place, you can face each workday with confidence, knowing every call, email, and meeting is a step toward the bigger vision you're building. The real power comes from showing up consistently, learning from setbacks, and letting your goals guide not just what you do, but why you do it.

Chapter 10:
Becoming a Leader

"I'm not sure I'm cut out for this leadership thing."

I must have said that a hundred times during my first year, thinking beyond my own sales numbers. And I meant it. The transformation from individual contributor to leader didn't happen overnight. It took decades, honestly. From the scared kid who could barely make eye contact with prospects to someone willing to knock on a customer's door demanding payment for a $40,000 invoice, the journey tested everything I thought I knew about myself.

Leadership isn't about a title or a new paycheck. It's about learning how to lift others and multiply success beyond your own reach. But here's what nobody tells you: It's also about getting comfortable being uncomfortable, having conversations that make your stomach turn, and standing firm when every instinct screams at you to back down.

In this chapter, I'll share what it really means to cross that line from top individual contributor to someone who influences an entire team—including the messy, difficult parts most leadership books skip.

From Top Performer to True Leader: The Transition Moment

Everything changed after my best month ever. I closed a deal so big it drew cheers from the team, even a congratulatory text from the VP. There was that burst of private pride—until the afterglow faded and something else took its place. I found myself scanning the sales leaderboard not for my name, but for a rep who'd been struggling. I caught myself thinking less about how many deals I closed and more about the nervous person next to me who actually needed my advice.

The shift from individual contributor to leader begins in those silent, split-second moments. Maybe it's when you hear someone fumble through a call and realize you know the answer, but aren't sure whether to step in. Maybe it happens after your big win, when a rookie asks how you did it, and you notice how much you want to see that "aha" look in their eyes. Pride and uncertainty mix together, and there's this sense that closing your own deals will never be enough again.

But here's where my story took a harder turn than I expected.

The Invoice That Changed Everything

I was riding high on my performance when my manager, Tom, pulled me aside one Tuesday morning. "Come with me," he said. "You need to see this part of the job."

We drove 40 minutes to a customer's warehouse—a client who'd been dodging calls about a $38,000 invoice that was 90 days overdue. I watched Tom walk through those doors with a calm I didn't understand yet, ask for the owner by name, and wait. When the owner finally appeared, making excuses about cash flow and payment schedules, Tom didn't flinch.

"I understand things are tight," Tom said, his voice steady but firm. "But we delivered everything we promised, on time. Your business depends on our partnership, and our business depends on getting paid. So, here's what's going to happen: You're going to write a check today for at least half, and we're going to schedule the rest."

I stood there sweating, watching this play out. The customer tried deflecting, tried negotiating, even tried to make Tom feel guilty. Tom didn't budge. Twenty minutes later, we walked out with a $20,000 check.

In the car, Tom turned to me. "Leadership isn't about being liked. It's about being responsible for the outcome—even when it's uncomfortable as hell."

That moment rewired something in my brain. I'd thought leadership was about inspiring people, sharing knowledge, and celebrating wins. And it is. But it's also about the conversations nobody wants to have. It's about standing in that warehouse, feeling your pulse race, and doing the hard thing anyway because the team's counting on you.

What Leadership Really Means

Leadership is not a new title pinned to your name or an extra zero on your paycheck. It's an expansion—of responsibility, perspective, and self-awareness. Before, the job was hitting your number. Now, it's about lifting the entire team's results, which includes the stuff that doesn't show up on motivational posters: chasing money, holding people accountable, and having difficult conversations.

Many top salespeople confuse leadership with authority or control, expecting to call every shot and bask in recognition. I sure did. But real leadership isn't about being in charge; it's about growing beyond yourself. That means confronting your own ego, breaking out of your habits, and accepting that sometimes you'll be the person standing in front of an angry customer demanding payment. It means choosing responsibility over comfort, every single time.

The challenge lies in letting your focus shift from the scoreboard you controlled to a much bigger, messier one—the one where your success is defined by how others grow under your wing (Asian Institute of Management, 2025). And here's the kicker: You have to protect that team by doing the hard parts of the job they can't see yet.

Leadership as Leverage—and Accountability

I learned that leadership is leverage, but not just the inspiring kind. When you multiply your knowledge across a team, your influence isn't just in how much you personally close but how much your team can do. Consider the math: one star salesperson might bring in $1 million a year. But a leader who shapes a team of five to each hit $500,000? That's $2.5 million, and growing.

But leverage also means you're the one who has to step up when things get uncomfortable. You're the one calling the client who's three months behind on payment. You're the one who has to tell a team member their performance isn't cutting it. You're the one who stays late to clean up the mess when a deal goes sideways.

Over the years, I went from being terrified of confrontation to understanding it as a core leadership skill. The scared kid who once avoided conflict learned to walk into offices, into tense meetings, into situations where someone needed to hear the truth—and deliver it with confidence. Not aggression. Not cruelty. But firmness.

The Two Brave Mindset Shifts

Stepping into leadership asks for two brave mindset shifts:

- **First:** Trading "How much did I sell?" for "How much did we achieve?"

- **Second:** Letting go of "How do I stand out?" and grabbing hold of "How do I help others shine?"

Both feel uncomfortable at first. The habits that got you to the top—competition, personal recognition—become less useful. There's real resistance when you have to cheer for a team member's win that outshines your own, or when your work is measured by group achievement, not just your stats.

But I'd add a third shift that nobody warned me about:

- **Third:** Trading "I want everyone to like me" for "I'm willing to be respected, even if it means being uncomfortable."

This one nearly broke me at first. I remember the first time I had to tell a customer we were pulling their credit line because they weren't paying. The person on the other end got angry, accused me of not understanding their situation, and tried to make me feel like the bad guy. Everything in me wanted to cave, to be "nice," to avoid the conflict. But I thought about Tom in that warehouse. I thought about my team depending on me to protect our business.

I didn't cave. And you know what? That customer paid. And respected me more afterward.

Leading Without Authority: Influence Through Action

You don't need a title to start leading others. True influence begins when you choose to set an example—staying prepared, tackling problems others avoid, showing integrity no matter who's watching.

Authority vs. Leadership

Authority is like a name tag. Anyone can get one when they move up the org chart, but not everyone leads with it. I've seen managers with fancy titles who bark orders and chase reports but never have anyone's back. People do the bare minimum "because the boss says so," and trust evaporates.

Then there's the senior rep with no direct reports, no office plaque, but when deals hit snags or pressure builds, everyone looks to them first. Their presence steadies the room. They drive action through influence, not control.

The lesson: Titles demand compliance; leadership earns real commitment (Linton, 2023).

The Power of Example—in the Hard Moments

People watch what you do, far more than what you say. When you get rejections, do you get flustered and blame others, or do you regroup and support the team without drama? When a colleague closes a huge sale, do you feel threatened or celebrate it as if it were your own?

But here's what I learned the hard way: People also watch how you handle confrontation. They watch when you have to make a difficult call to a customer who's been avoiding you. They watch when you need to hold someone accountable for missing a deadline. They watch when you have to deliver bad news or make an unpopular decision.

I remember when a team member kept making excuses for missed quotas—good excuses, too. Personal stuff, market conditions, bad leads. All technically true. But week after week, nothing changed. Everyone on the team was watching to see what I'd do. Would I be the "cool" leader who let it slide? Or would I step up?

I pulled him aside privately and said, "I see what you're dealing with, and I respect the challenges. But here's the truth: You're capable of more than this, and we both know it. So what's it going to take for you to turn this around?" That conversation was harder than any cold call I'd ever made. But it changed everything. He respected the directness. Performance improved. And the rest of the team saw that accountability wasn't personal—it was professional.

Three Practical Ways to Lead Without a Title

Take Initiative in Murky Moments

Be the first to take initiative when there's murkiness or challenge in the group. If a project is stuck, volunteer to map out next steps or find common ground. Use language like: "I've been thinking about a couple solutions. Do you mind if I sketch them out for us?" People crave direction in tough moments.

Share Credit Publicly, Take Responsibility Privately

When things go well: "Erin handled the negotiation that actually swung this deal." When things go sideways, own the team result and talk solutions. Don't name anyone else at the debrief. This approach gathers supporters fast (Cabuyao, 2023).

Stand Firm When It Matters

This is the one most people miss. Leadership isn't just about being helpful—it's about standing your ground when you know you're right. I learned this collecting money, but it applies everywhere. When a customer demands an unreasonable discount, when a team member tries to cut corners, when someone pushes back on a standard you've set—stand firm. Calm, professional, but immovable. That's when people start to really follow you.

Earning Respect Through Daily Leadership

A leadership badge doesn't carry weight if people don't respect you. Respect isn't something you demand; it's a daily scorecard quietly kept by everyone around you, measuring how you show up. If you want people to follow your lead, they have to want to, not just because it's their job but because they believe in what you bring to the table.

The Three Pillars of Respect

Three pillars build that foundation: competence, consistency, and character.

- **Competence** means staying hungry and curious. Step into tough client meetings with clarity. Coach a rep through a new objection on the fly. Admit what you don't know and invite the team to learn with you. The more people see you rolling up your sleeves, the more they'll trust you.

- **Consistency** is the pillar where most leaders lose their teams. It's about whether you do what you say—every time. Send a clear email and stick by it. Back a rep's risk and don't cut them loose when it gets tricky. Show up on hard days, not just good ones. When your responses are predictable and fair, people feel safe bringing you problems they can't solve alone.

- **Character** shows when you face choices that cost you something. It's easy to make the right call when it doesn't affect your commission. But how do you act when the ethical route slows you down, or requires you to own a mistake? Character shows in the meetings no one else attends, the feedback you give honestly but kindly, and taking responsibility when something goes wrong before anyone calls you out.

The Practice of Walking the Floor

One practice that unites all three pillars is "walking the floor." Get out from behind your desk. Be where your team is. Notice the nervous energy before a big pitch, see the frustration after a rough call, ask "How's that account shaping up?" and offer suggestions in real-time.

I learned this from Tom. He never sat in his office when the team was struggling. He'd walk past your desk, notice something was off, and pull up a chair. Not to micromanage, but to be present. It made all the difference.

When Respect Gets Tested

Even with all this, you'll face moments when respect slips—or you feel it being tested. Maybe someone challenges your decision in front of the team, or a mistake gets blamed on your call.

Instead of firing back, pause. Take a breath. Listen. Aim to understand their point of view. Invite the conversation. Stay calm. By tackling disrespect with maturity, you model grace under pressure, and sometimes win more respect from those moments than from all your wins combined.

I think about the time I had to chase down a $42,000 invoice from a customer who'd been ghosting us for weeks. When I finally got him on the phone, he exploded—accused me of harassment, threatened to take his business elsewhere, and said I was being unreasonable. Old me would have backed down immediately. But I'd learned by then that leadership means holding the line.

"I understand you're frustrated," I said. "But we fulfilled our end of the agreement. Your account is important to us, which is exactly why we need to get this resolved. I'm happy to work out a payment plan, but walking away from the obligation isn't an option."

He hung up on me. My hands were shaking. But an hour later, he called back and agreed to the payment plan. And the team, who'd been watching to see if I'd fold, saw what leadership really looked like. Not aggression. Not being a pushover either. Just steady, confident accountability.

Mentorship: The Growth Multiplier

Once you've built trust through showing up consistently and standing firm when it matters, you can move into genuine mentorship—where guidance becomes the most effective tool for multiplying your influence.

Why Mentorship Matters

Think back on the people who shaped your best habits or taught you how to handle disappointment. They weren't just fountains of advice; they helped you see yourself as capable of leveling up. That's where mentorship often gets misunderstood—it isn't one-way. You provide direction and lessons learned, but your mentees bring fresh perspectives that can jolt you out of ruts (DSpace, 2025).

Starting With Listening

Becoming an effective mentor starts with listening. Great mentors pause and ask real questions first: "What's been your toughest call lately?" or "Where do you feel out of your depth?" This turns mentorship from a lecture into a conversation.

I remember when a junior rep came to me after losing a big deal. Rather than immediately offering solutions, I asked, "Walk me through what happened. How did you feel going in?" This let her process the experience and gave me the starting point for teaching.

Encouraging Independence and Building Systems

Avoid becoming the answer machine. If someone asks, "Should I take this client call alone?" flip it: "What would an experienced rep do in your shoes?" Celebrate effort—an improved cold call, a creative follow-up. The best breakthroughs come when a mentee realizes they're trusted and supported, not micromanaged.

To magnify this effect, create teachable systems. Informal mentoring isn't enough—your expertise needs a framework. Design a quick morning check-in where everyone shares one challenge. Start a ritual where, after every closed deal, the team does a 10-minute debrief. Outline your favorite approach so others can adapt it (DSpace, 2025).

The Leadership Paradox

Here's the counterintuitive law: Every time you share your expertise, your influence doesn't shrink—it expands. I trained a new rep who quickly picked up speed and started to outsell me. Old-school thinking might see this as competition. But I celebrated it. Her win was evidence that mentorship worked. When you invest generously in others, your own impact grows wider and stronger (DSpace, 2025). Leadership that multiplies is built on abundance, not scarcity.

The Emotional Side: From Scarcity to Abundance

The way you show up as a leader changes when you stop seeing knowledge as currency to hide and start treating it as something to share so others can grow strong around you.

The old scarcity mindset keeps your best contacts close, shares only the minimum, and treats teammates as rivals. Result? A team divided, momentum lost as everyone spins alone.

The abundance shift feels risky at first. You wonder if helping others will water down your achievements. But when you flip the switch—when you celebrate another rep's closed deal, plug a teammate's fresh approach, hand out your "secret" template—you see trust bloom.

The Leadership Mirror and Emotional Discipline

Once you measure yourself by your team's success, you'll notice leadership holds up a mirror to your blind spots. Your reactions—those first flashes of frustration, disappointment, self-justification—show up in your tone, your words, even how long you pause before replying.

Emotional intelligence comes down to whether you react or respond. Reacting impulsively might mean firing off a defensive reply or snapping at your team. Responding thoughtfully means taking a breath, asking a clarifying question, and turning the situation into a learning moment.

Your mood sets the weather for the whole team. If you stay steady during a rough patch, you give others permission to bring you problems without fear. If you storm, they shut down.

I learned this the hard way. Early in my leadership journey, I'd get visibly frustrated when things went wrong. The team started hiding problems from me, which made everything worse. When I finally learned to pause, breathe, and respond instead of react, everything shifted. Problems got surfaced earlier. Solutions came faster. Trust deepened.

Redefining Success and Building Legacy

Winning used to be about my stats and my check. Over time, the thrill of ringing the sales bell alone faded—but seeing someone I mentored score a big deal? That stuck around.

I think about mentoring Sarah, who struggled with cold calling. I spent weeks practicing with her, shared my follow-up templates, and talked through her anxieties. The day she landed her first major client, the pride on her face changed her whole path. For me, her win felt bigger than any personal deal. I'd taught her how to keep growing, even when I wasn't looking over her shoulder.

That's leadership legacy: The wins your people keep stacking up, long after you step back.

The Evolution Never Stops

From the scared kid who couldn't handle confrontation to the person willing to stand firm in a warehouse demanding payment—that evolution took decades, and honestly, it's still happening. Every tough conversation teaches me something. Every time I have to choose between being liked and being respected, I get a little better at making the right call.

Leadership isn't about comfort. It's about responsibility. It's about doing the hard thing because your team's counting on you. It's about holding the line when customers avoid you, having the difficult conversations, standing firm on standards, and multiplying success through others, even when it costs you something.

Action Steps for Sustainable Leadership

To put what we talked about above into action, here are three challenges you should strongly consider:

- **Model one new behavior this week:** Choose to be fully transparent in how you make a decision, or admit a mistake publicly so others learn it's safe to do the same.

- **Pick one mentee:** Name a teammate who's hungry to learn. Teach them your go-to method for handling objections, and schedule regular check-ins to watch their growth.

- **Practice one difficult conversation:** Identify something that needs addressing—an unpaid invoice, a missed deadline, or underperformance. Plan the conversation, stay calm and firm, and follow through. Your team is watching how you handle the uncomfortable moments.

Wrapping It Up

Leadership isn't about titles or personal glory; it's about lifting your whole team and creating a culture where everyone wins together. But it's also about the messy, uncomfortable stuff: having hard conversations, demanding accountability, standing firm when customers push back, and choosing responsibility over comfort.

The real win comes when you see others grow, thrive, and surpass what you once thought was the limit. Your journey from solo star to true leader starts with one brave choice: to step into the uncomfortable conversations, to stand firm when it matters, and to multiply your success through others.

So, take that first step: Share your knowledge freely, listen deeply, hold people accountable with respect, and celebrate the victories of those around you. Your impact will echo far beyond any single deal—because you had the courage to lead when it wasn't easy.

Chapter 11:
Leaders and Followers—Finding Your Rhythm in Sales

"Wait, so sometimes I need to follow instead of lead?"

That question stopped me cold during a sales meeting years ago. I'd shown up ready to take charge, full of ideas and brimming with confidence, only to realize the real power wasn't in pushing my own voice forward; it was in knowing when to listen, step back, and support the people around me.

It was a humbling lesson. And honestly? It turned out to be the secret behind every strong sales team I've been part of since.

But here's what I learned that went even deeper than team dynamics: In every interaction—whether with customers, prospects, teammates, or managers—there is always a leader and a follower. Always. No exceptions.

Understanding that fundamental truth changes everything about how you approach sales. Because if you don't consciously choose to lead the conversation, the customer will lead it for you. And when that happens, you've already lost.

The Core Truth: Every Interaction Has a Leader and a Follower

The Moment I Understood

Early in my sales career, I walked into a meeting with a prospect who seemed friendly enough. We chatted. We laughed. The conversation felt easy and natural. I left feeling great about our connection.

And then nothing happened. No sale. No follow-up. No momentum.

I couldn't figure out what went wrong until my manager pulled me aside and asked one simple question: "Who was leading that conversation—you or the customer?"

I replayed the meeting in my head. The customer had asked all the questions. Set the pace. Determined which topics we discussed and for how long. Decided when the meeting ended. I'd been so focused on being likable and building rapport that I'd completely abdicated my responsibility to lead.

I wasn't selling. I was just... being there. Reacting. Responding. Following.

That's when I realized the fundamental principle that would transform my entire approach to sales: In every interaction, someone leads, and someone follows. The leader directs the tone, controls the confidence level, and determines the flow of the conversation. The follower reacts, hesitates, and responds to whatever direction the leader sets.

What Leadership Actually Means in Sales

Leadership in a sales context isn't about being domineering or pushy. It's about taking responsibility for the direction and outcome of the conversation.

A leader walks into a meeting knowing what needs to happen. They set the agenda. They control the emotional temperature of the room. They guide the prospect through a journey that leads to a clear decision point—not through manipulation, but through clarity and confidence.

A follower, on the other hand, lets the prospect dictate everything. They wait to see what the customer wants to talk about. They respond to objections defensively rather than addressing them proactively. They ask, "What do you think?" when they should be saying, "Here's what I recommend."

Think about the best salespeople you've ever encountered—the ones who made buying feel effortless and natural. I guarantee they were leading the interaction from the first moment. They knew where the conversation was going, and they guided you there with such skill that you barely noticed you were being led.

The Psychology of Conversational Dominance

There's actual psychology behind this concept. Research shows that in any social interaction, people unconsciously establish dominance hierarchies within the first few minutes (*Followership: The Cinderella of Leadership*, 2025). This happens through subtle cues: who speaks first, whose ideas get deferred to, who sets the emotional tone, who controls the pacing.

In sales conversations, this dynamic is even more pronounced because both parties know that something transactional is at stake. The customer is trying to evaluate whether they should trust you and your solution. You're trying to guide them toward a decision that genuinely benefits them.

If you show up uncertain, reactive, or apologetic in your energy, the customer's brain registers you as the follower. Once that happens, they start leading—asking skeptical questions, raising objections, controlling the timeline, and ultimately deciding not to buy because they never felt confident in your ability to deliver.

But when you show up with quiet certainty, clear direction, and genuine enthusiasm for how you can help them, their brain registers you as the leader. They relax. They trust. They follow your guidance because you've demonstrated through your presence that you know where you're going.

The Trap of Customer-Led Conversations

Here's what happens when you let the customer lead: They will inevitably lead you toward inaction.

Why? Because most customers' default mode is caution. They're worried about making mistakes. They're concerned about spending money unwisely. They're skeptical because they've been burned before.

If you let that cautious, skeptical energy drive the conversation, you end up in an endless loop of questions, objections, and "Let me think about it." The sale dies not because your solution wasn't good enough, but because nobody was confident enough to lead the prospect toward a decision.

I learned this the hard way dozens of times before it finally clicked. I'd walk into meetings prepared to answer whatever questions came my way, thinking that being responsive and accommodating was the path to success.

But responsiveness without leadership is just passivity in disguise. The customer would ask questions, and I'd answer them. They'd raise concerns, and I'd address them. But at the end, they'd say they needed more time to think, and I'd agree because I didn't want to seem pushy.

What I failed to understand was that they weren't asking for more time because they needed it; they were asking because I hadn't given them a confident reason to move forward right then.

How Scripts, Tone, and Excitement Create "Follower Mode" in Customers

The Power of Scripted Confidence

Once I understood the leader-follower dynamic, I started paying attention to what actually put customers into "follower mode," that state where they trust your direction and follow your lead naturally.

Three elements emerged as absolutely critical: scripts, tone, and excitement.

First, scripts. And I know what you're thinking. *Scripts sound robotic and inauthentic.* But here's what I discovered: Having a script doesn't mean you sound scripted. It means you've done the mental work in advance so you can be fully present in the moment.

When I walked into meetings without a clear script—just "winging it" based on how I felt—I was actually putting myself in follower mode. I was reacting to whatever the customer brought up rather than leading them through a proven journey.

But when I had a clear script—not word-for-word, but a proven structure for how I'd open, build value, handle objections, and close—I showed up as a leader. The customer could feel that I'd done this before, that I knew what came next, that they were in capable hands.

Your script is your roadmap. It's the evidence to yourself and your prospect that you're the expert guiding this journey, not a passenger hoping things work out.

Tone: The Invisible Controller

Tone is even more powerful than words. I can say the exact same sentence with two different tones and get completely opposite results.

"This solution could really work for you," said with uncertainty and a questioning inflection, puts the customer in charge. They hear the doubt. They start questioning whether it really would work.

"This solution is going to work perfectly for you," said with calm certainty and a declarative tone, creates followership. They hear the confidence. They believe it because you believe it.

During my $50-a-week period, I learned that tone was one of the few things that cost absolutely nothing but delivered massive returns. I couldn't afford fancy presentation materials or elaborate client dinners. But I could control my tone.

I practiced in the mirror. I recorded myself on sales calls and listened back, cringing at every moment of uncertainty in my voice. I worked on eliminating uptalk—that habit of ending statements like questions—because it surrendered leadership every single time.

The transformation was remarkable. When I started speaking with declarative certainty—even about the same products, to similar customers—my close rate jumped. Not because the offering changed, but because my tone told customers I was leading and they could trust that leadership.

Excitement: The Emotional Transfer

The third element is excitement, and this might be the most misunderstood aspect of sales leadership.

Some people think excitement means being loud or hyperactive. That's not what I mean. Excitement is genuine enthusiasm for how your solution will improve your customer's life or business.

When you're truly excited about what you're offering, that emotion transfers. Emotions are contagious. Research on emotional contagion shows that people unconsciously mirror the emotional states of those around them, especially those they perceive as leaders (Asian Institute of Management, 2025).

If you're bored, uncertain, or apologetic about your product, the customer feels that and mirrors it back. They become skeptical, disengaged, or critical.

But if you're genuinely excited—if you believe deeply that what you're offering will make their life better—they feel that, too. Your excitement becomes their curiosity, then their interest, then their desire to buy.

I remember a specific turning point in my career when I stopped trying to be "professional" in that stiff, corporate way and started letting my genuine excitement show. I was selling a solution I truly believed in, and instead of tamping down my enthusiasm to seem more serious, I let it shine through.

"I'm honestly excited to show you this because I think it's going to solve that exact problem you mentioned" became my authentic opening. And customers responded by leaning in, getting excited themselves, and making decisions faster.

The Formula: Scripts + Tone + Excitement = Leadership

When you combine all three elements—a proven script that provides structure, a confident tone that conveys certainty, and genuine excitement that creates emotional transfer—you create what I call "automatic leadership."

The customer immediately registers you as the expert, the guide, the person who knows what's next. They slide naturally into follower mode, not because you've manipulated them, but because you've made it clear through every element of your presence that you're capable of leading them to the right decision.

This doesn't mean you ignore their concerns or railroad them into buying something they don't need. True leadership in sales means guiding people toward decisions that genuinely serve them. But you have to lead that process, or it won't happen.

If You Don't Lead, the Customer Will—And You Lose

The Uncomfortable Truth

Here's the uncomfortable truth I had to face: Most sales are lost not because the product wasn't right or the price was too high, but because the salesperson failed to lead.

When you don't take charge of the conversation, the customer does. And when the customer leads, they almost always lead toward not buying.

Why? Because buying requires overcoming natural resistance. It requires moving past fear, uncertainty, and the human default toward maintaining the status quo. Customers almost never lead themselves through that discomfort—they need you to guide them.

Think about a time you were the customer in an important buying decision. Maybe you were looking at houses, or cars, or considering a major service. The salespeople who got your business weren't the ones who asked what you wanted and then disappeared. They were the ones who confidently showed you options, addressed your concerns before you raised them, and guided you toward a decision that felt right.

The ones who lost your business probably asked a lot of questions, seemed very accommodating, and ultimately left you feeling like you were in this alone—that you had to figure everything out yourself and take all the risk.

What Customer-Led Conversations Look Like

Customer-led conversations follow a predictable pattern. The customer asks questions, you answer. They raise objections, you respond. They say they need to think about it, you agree and hope they'll come back.

At every decision point, you're waiting for them to tell you what happens next. And because they're in leader mode—and they don't want to buy from someone who seems less confident than they are—they lead you straight to "no thanks."

I used to think I was being respectful and consultative by letting customers drive. I'd say things like, "What would you like to know?" or "What questions do you have for me?" or "When would be a good time for you to make a decision?"

Every one of those questions gave away leadership. They told the customer that I was following their lead, waiting for their direction, and depending on them to move the process forward.

Taking Back Leadership

The shift happened when I started structuring conversations completely differently. Instead of asking what they wanted to know, I said, "Let me walk you through how this works and how it's going to solve that challenge you mentioned."

Instead of asking when they wanted to decide, I said, "Based on your timeline, we should move forward by Friday to make sure you have this in place for your launch. Does morning or afternoon work better for you?"

Instead of responding to objections, I started addressing them preemptively: "Now, you might be wondering about the price compared to competitor X. Here's why our solution actually costs you less in the long run..."

These weren't manipulative tactics. They were me taking responsibility for leading the conversation toward an outcome that served the customer. And the results were dramatic.

Customers stopped saying, "Let me think about it" because I'd already structured the conversation to address their thinking during our time together. They stopped raising unexpected objections because I'd covered them before they became obstacles. They started buying because I'd made it clear, through confident leadership, that buying was the right decision.

The Team Dynamic: Leading and Following

Now, here's where it gets interesting. Everything I've said about leading customers also applies to team dynamics, but with a critical twist: In teams, you have to know when to lead and when to follow.

With customers, you should almost always be leading. With teammates, true excellence comes from fluid movement between the two roles.

I learned this the hard way during that early sales meeting I mentioned at the beginning of this chapter. I showed up trying to lead, even though everyone in the room had more expertise than I did. I should have been following—learning from the veterans, asking thoughtful questions, supporting their proven strategies.

But over time, as I developed my own expertise in certain areas, I learned to step into leadership confidently when my knowledge or perspective could serve the team. And I learned to step back just as confidently when someone else had the better approach.

The Dance: Understanding How Leadership and Followership Work Together in Teams

Two Halves of One Heartbeat

Leadership and followership aren't locked in some rigid hierarchy where one is always above the other. They're partners, like the two halves of a heartbeat that keep momentum moving forward.

Leaders provide vision—someone sets the destination, frames the goal, and injects energy into the team. Followers channel that energy into disciplined action: organizing systems, pushing initiatives forward, clarifying details, and making the difficult calls.

You see this at the start of every sales cycle. The team leader rallies everyone with a new target, paints a picture of what's possible, and sets expectations for the quarter. Then the rest of the group gets to work: tracking KPIs, analyzing call results, testing scripts, and bringing up ideas the leader might have missed.

In this give and take, the leader learns when to listen and when to guide. The team learns when to question and when to trust. Like a dance, there's an unspoken agreement—one partner leads this step, the other supports and follows, then the roles switch (*Followership: The Cinderella of Leadership*, 2025).

Fluid Leadership in Practice

Here's where things get really interesting for modern sales teams: fluid leadership. Instead of sticking to a rigid organizational chart, you let the person with the most relevant skill or idea take the lead for that particular moment.

Say your team has a new product update, and Cassidy—your quiet, detail-obsessed solutions rep—has run every customer Q&A session for the past two quarters. Why not have her walk everyone through best practices this time?

People will listen more closely because she's the expert. And Cassidy steps into a leadership role, gaining confidence and visibility she might never get otherwise.

Every time you step aside and let another expert shine, you're building trust and giving everyone a stake in the team's success. That's where you find the real competitive edge: when everyone knows they might lead tomorrow, so they support the person leading today.

Reading the Room

Knowing when to step forward and when to support someone else takes self-awareness—understanding yourself, your team, and the situation in front of you.

Think about those moments when you look around the room and see uncertainty in your group, but you know what comes next. Maybe you see a junior teammate freeze when a customer objects to pricing. If you feel that pull inside to say something or organize the next steps—and you're acting from a genuine desire to help, not ego—that's your signal to step up.

But leadership isn't always the best choice. Sometimes, the strongest thing you can do is recognize when someone else has the advantage—and support them fully. Maybe you have a colleague who built killer rapport with an important prospect. In those cases, insisting on your own idea for the sake of proving yourself only muddies the water and risks fracturing trust (Cabuyao, 2023).

Your best move? Reinforce the plan, cover the blind spots for your partner, and give your undivided attention to flawless execution.

Passing It On: How Mentorship Creates a Self-Renewing Team

The Living Cycle

Once you've figured out the rhythm of leading and following in your own sales role, the next level is showing others how to find it too. That shift marks the move from personal mastery to true leadership.

Most of the time, you're not delivering some epic lesson. You're just doing your work, showing people what steady, effective selling looks like day after day.

People watch you way closer than you realize. Sales teams operate like training grounds. Everyone is always learning, especially by observing the people one step ahead of them. Over time, you start to notice when someone on your team uses your exact wording on a discovery call. You see them walk into a meeting with the same confident posture you've been modeling.

Not long ago, I watched one of our newer reps run a high-stakes demo. He kicked things off with the same opening story I'd used in a training session weeks earlier. But then I heard him tweak my line about pricing—he made it sharper, more confident. You could see the client lean in, fully engaged.

I felt a rush of pride mixed with pressure. My habits—good and bad—were shaping what "good" looked like for him. Maybe for the whole team.

The Shadow Leadership Day

There's a practical tool that cuts months off the development process: the "shadow leadership day."

Identify someone ready to stretch. Assign them a real leadership task—leading the morning huddle, designing a key pitch, or managing a client escalation. Prep them thoroughly, then hand them the keys and let them lead while you observe silently.

Debrief honestly afterward. Highlight what worked, where their process could tighten up, and what surprised you. Then rotate the opportunity to different rising players on your team.

When you turn leadership from something hidden and mysterious into something built into daily work, you make growth feel possible for everyone.

Channeling Competition: Keeping the Fire Without the Fracture

The Paradox

Sales teams are full of people who love to win. Here's the paradox: Competition pushes your team to new heights, but if it turns into an every-person-for-themselves battle, you get hidden resentment, information hoarding, and a culture that quietly falls apart (Workplace Insights, 2024).

You can't stomp out competition. It's the rocket fuel of sales, but you have to steer it.

Compete With Yesterday

Start with the "compete with yesterday" mindset. The only rivalry you want to encourage is against the version of yourself from last week. Make it normal for everyone to track their own numbers and challenge themselves to beat them, instead of trying to edge out the person at the next desk.

When a rep hits a personal best, celebrate that milestone with the focus squarely on "personal best," not "beating Steve." The team keeps getting better because each person's competitive fire is pointed uphill toward improvement, not sideways at their teammates.

Rewire Success Perception

Fundamentally rewire how people see each other's successes. Most sales professionals arrive hardwired to see a teammate's big win as somehow a loss for themselves. You have to actively teach the flip: See every win as a how-to manual available for everyone.

When someone lands the huge account, dig in. Ask them to share how they approached the prospect, what they said, and what obstacles they overcame. Break down those victories and make this part of your regular team rhythm.

The Secret Weapon: Humility and Empowerment

The Paradox That Changes Everything

Here's a paradox that sounds simple but runs counter to almost everything we're taught: The most powerful leaders are those humble enough to follow.

When leadership became a shared identity on my team—not just a rank or title—everything about our chemistry and results changed. Humility emerged as my secret weapon—the force that made my influence expand rather than shrink.

Humility keeps you teachable. When you make it a habit to listen more than you speak during team meetings, you build real loyalty. The best meetings I've ever led started with a question: "What do you think we should do next?"

The Empowerment Formula

The empowerment formula is elegantly clear: Trust + Tools + Autonomy = Ownership.

Trust means you believe in your people loudly and often. Tools are the resources and training to do the job without constant hand-holding. Autonomy is real permission to make decisions and take calculated risks.

Once, a major client nearly walked because of a miscommunication on our end. Ordinarily, I would have jumped in immediately. Instead, I let a newer teammate—Jess—take the lead. She knew the client's concerns intimately.

Jess owned our shortcomings directly and proposed a solution the client loved—something I wouldn't have thought of. The relationship was saved, the client doubled their orders, and Jess became the go-to person for troubleshooting tough relationships.

By supporting her rise rather than taking the rescue role myself, my influence stretched farther than it ever could through personal heroics.

Wrapping It Up

Now that we've uncovered the dance between leading and following, it's clear that sales success isn't about who's in charge; it's about how well you understand when to lead and when to follow.

With customers, lead almost always. Direct the tone, control the flow, and guide them confidently toward decisions that serve them. Use scripts, tone, and genuine excitement to put them in follower mode naturally.

With teams, master the fluid movement between roles. Step up with confidence when your expertise serves the group. Step back with humility when someone else has the better approach.

Remember the core philosophy: In every interaction, there is a leader and a follower. The question isn't whether this dynamic exists—it's whether you'll consciously choose which role serves the moment best.

Chapter 12:
Mastering a Strong Sales Mindset and Developing Mental Toughness

Sales isn't just about knowing your product inside and out or having a pitch so smooth it could sell ice to penguins. It's about what's happening inside your head long before you pick up that phone or walk into that meeting.

The real challenge? Handling rejection without letting it destroy you. Managing doubt when it whispers in your ear at 2 a.m. Staying confident when every single thing seems stacked against you.

Here's the brutal truth: If your mindset cracks under pressure, no amount of preparation will save the deal.

But here's what I discovered during my journey from making $50 a week to building a thriving sales career: Mental toughness isn't just about surviving the hard days. It's about showing up with so much energy, personality, and genuine excitement that customers can't help but be drawn in. Because at the end of the day, people don't buy products. They buy excitement. They buy the experience you create.

This chapter takes a hard look at how to build genuine mental toughness while developing a sales mindset that turns every interaction into a performance worth remembering.

The Battle You Fight Before Anyone Says Hello

Why Mental Armor Isn't Optional

Every deal you close and every deal you lose is decided long before the pitch even starts.

You might have memorized the script perfectly. You've practiced your objection handling until you can do it in your sleep. But none of that will save you if your belief system folds at the first sign of trouble.

As I mentioned in previous chapters, I learned this during my early days when I was barely surviving on commission. The mental game wasn't optional—it was everything. Because when you're that hungry, you can't afford to let doubt win.

So many salespeople fall for the old myth that product knowledge or slick technique guarantees success. You see it every single week: Someone walks in Monday morning with a solid plan and a clear quota, then vanishes by Friday because they couldn't stomach another "not interested."

The hard truth? Sales is a battle inside your own head before you ever face a prospect.

Who Really Wins in Sales

The masters aren't the ones with the sharpest pitch or the fanciest slide deck. They're the ones relentless enough to sell belief, confidence, and persistence to themselves every single morning—long before a customer ever hears their voice.

But here's what I learned that goes beyond just surviving: The real winners are the ones who bring so much energy and entertainment value to their presentations that customers remember them long after the meeting ends.

It's More About Emotions, Less About Products

The Truth Nobody Tells You

Here's something that took me years to fully understand: Customers don't buy products. They buy the excitement you create around those products.

Think about it. When was the last time you made a significant purchase—a car, a phone, a service—based purely on a spec sheet? Probably never. You bought it because someone made you feel excited about what owning it would mean for your life.

During my early sales career, I was so focused on memorizing product features and benefits that I forgot the most important thing: Nobody cares about features until they're emotionally invested. And emotional investment comes from excitement, entertainment, and energy.

I remember the exact moment this clicked for me. I was watching a veteran salesperson who consistently outsold everyone else on the team. His product knowledge was actually worse than mine. His pitch wasn't any more polished. But he had something I didn't: He made every presentation feel like an event.

He walked in with energy that filled the room. He told stories that made prospects laugh. He turned product demonstrations into performances that people actually enjoyed watching. While I was droning through feature lists, he was creating an experience.

And he closed deals I couldn't touch.

I studied him obsessively for weeks. What was he doing that I wasn't? The answer became clear: He understood that selling was theater. Not in a fake or manipulative way, but in the sense that great theater engages emotions, tells compelling stories, and creates moments people remember long after the curtain falls.

He didn't just explain what the product did—he painted vivid pictures of what life would be like after the customer bought. He didn't just answer objections—he told stories about other customers who had the same concerns and were now thrilled they took the leap. He didn't just close deals—he created experiences that made customers want to say yes.

That realization changed everything for me. I stopped trying to be the most knowledgeable person in the room and started focusing on being the most engaging.

Entertainment as Part of Selling

That's when I realized: Entertainment isn't separate from selling. It's essential to it.

This doesn't mean you become a clown or turn your pitch into a comedy routine. It means you recognize that holding attention, creating emotional resonance, and making your presentation memorable are skills as important as knowing your close rates.

I started experimenting. Instead of starting meetings with the standard "Thanks for your time today," I'd walk in with something unexpected: "I'm genuinely excited to show you this—I think you're going to love what we've built."

The energy shift was immediate. People leaned in instead of leaning back.

Instead of listing features, I started telling stories: "Last month, one of our clients was struggling with exactly what you described. Here's what happened when they implemented this solution..."

People remembered those stories. They repeated them to colleagues. They made decisions based on them.

I also learned to read the room and adjust my performance accordingly. Some customers wanted high energy and enthusiasm. Others preferred a more measured, consultative approach. The key was understanding that both were performances—I was still consciously choosing how to show up based on what would resonate most with that particular audience.

Think of the best teachers you ever had. They didn't just convey information—they made learning engaging. They used humor, stories, demonstrations, and energy to keep you interested. That's exactly what great salespeople do. They understand that education without entertainment leads to boredom, and bored customers don't buy.

I started treating my sales presentations like I was hosting a show. Not in a way that felt forced or artificial, but with the understanding that I had a responsibility to make the experience worth my customer's time. If they were going to give me 30 minutes or an hour, I owed them more than just facts and figures. I owed them an experience that left them feeling informed, engaged, and excited about what was possible.

Personality Layered Over the Script

As I mentioned in earlier chapters about leadership and followership, having a script is crucial. But here's what I learned about scripts: They're the foundation, not the performance.

Your personality needs to be layered over every scripted element. The words might be the same from one presentation to the next, but the energy, the emphasis, the moments of humor or passion—those should be authentically you.

I started bringing my whole personality to every interaction. If something struck me as funny, I laughed. If I was genuinely impressed by a customer's operation, I said so with real enthusiasm. If I believed deeply that my solution would transform their business, I let that conviction show in my voice and body language.

The script became a skeleton I dressed with my personality, energy, and genuine excitement about helping customers win.

Creating Memorable Experiences Through Playfulness

Superhero Nicknames and Personal Branding

Here's something that might sound silly but worked incredibly well: I started giving myself playful internal identities depending on the type of call or meeting I was walking into.

Tough negotiation? I was "The Closer." Complicated technical demo? I became "The Wizard." Customer having a bad day? "The Problem Solver" showed up.

These weren't names I necessarily shared with customers (though sometimes I did, in the right context with the right humor). They were mental switches that helped me step into the energy and persona that situation needed.

Think about superheroes: They don't just have powers; they have identities that shape how they show up. Batman brings intensity and preparation. Spider-Man brings wit and agility. When I started thinking about sales roles the same way, it helped me bring the right energy to each situation.

The beauty of this approach was that it made the mental shift from "me" to "sales professional" feel more intentional. Instead of just showing up and hoping I'd have the right energy, I consciously chose which version of myself the situation called for.

Eventually, some of these playful identities became part of my actual brand. Customers started introducing me to colleagues as "the guy who always brings the energy" or "the salesperson who actually makes meetings fun." That reputation preceded me and opened doors.

One client even started calling me by one of my internal nicknames after I jokingly mentioned it during a relaxed moment in a meeting. It became a running joke between us, and that playful rapport made our business relationship stronger. He sent me more referrals than any other client that year—not because my product was better, but because the experience of working with me was memorable and enjoyable.

The lesson? Don't be afraid to bring your personality, and even playfulness, to your professional interactions. People do business with people they like and remember. Being memorable doesn't require being outrageous. It just requires being willing to show up as a full human being, not a corporate robot.

Turning Product Features Into Performances

I completely transformed how I handled product demonstrations. Instead of clicking through slides and explaining features, I turned them into shows.

For physical products, I'd create moments of drama: "Watch what happens when..." For services, I'd use storytelling to paint vivid pictures: "Imagine it's Monday morning, you walk into your office, and instead of the usual chaos, everything just flows because this system is handling..."

I started using props, metaphors, and unexpected demonstrations. I'd compare complex processes to things people already understood— sports plays, cooking recipes, even movie plots. Anything to make the abstract concrete and the boring memorable.

The goal wasn't just to inform; it was to entertain while informing. To create an experience people wanted to be part of rather than endure.

One of my most effective techniques was what I called "the reveal." Instead of front-loading all the impressive features, I'd build to them. I'd start with the problem, create some tension around why it mattered, and then—at just the right moment—reveal how our solution handled it in a way that often surprised and delighted prospects.

"Now, you might be wondering how we handle that issue without creating more work for your team. Here's where it gets interesting..."

And then I'd demonstrate the feature in a way that felt like unwrapping a gift rather than checking a box on a feature list.

I also learned to use silence strategically. After demonstrating something impressive, I'd pause. Let it sink in. Watch their faces register what they'd just seen. That moment of silence created space for the impact to hit, rather than rushing past it to the next feature.

Turning features into performances also meant being willing to improvise. If a customer asked an unexpected question, instead of just answering verbally, I'd often demonstrate the answer in real time. "Great question! Let me show you exactly how that works." This spontaneous demonstration often impressed them more than my prepared content because it showed genuine mastery, not just memorized talking points.

Bringing Emotional Energy to Presentations

Energy is contagious. As I learned in previous chapters about emotional contagion, the energy you bring to an interaction becomes the baseline for everyone else in the room.

I made a conscious decision: I would always bring more energy than seemed necessary. Not fake energy—genuine enthusiasm rooted in my belief that what I was offering would genuinely help.

This meant managing my own state carefully before every interaction. I'd take a moment to get my body activated—do some jumping jacks, listen to music that pumped me up, or simply stand in a power pose for a few minutes.

Then, I'd walk into the room like I was genuinely excited to be there. Because I was. Every meeting was an opportunity to help someone, to build a relationship, to demonstrate my value. Why wouldn't I be excited about that?

Customers responded by matching that energy. Meetings that might have been stiff and formal became collaborative and dynamic. People smiled more. They engaged more. They bought more.

But here's what I learned about energy: It's not just about volume or hyperactivity. Sometimes, the most powerful energy is calm confidence. Sometimes, it's quiet intensity. The key is being fully present and emotionally engaged, whatever form that takes.

I remember one particularly important meeting with a skeptical executive who'd been burned by salespeople before. Walking in with high energy would have backtracked immediately—he would have seen it as more sales BS. Instead, I brought what I call "focused intensity." I sat forward, made steady eye contact, spoke clearly and deliberately, and demonstrated through my presence that I was taking him and his concerns seriously.

That focused energy—that sense of "I'm fully here with you"—broke through his defenses far more effectively than any enthusiastic pitch would have. He later told me that what sold him was that I seemed to genuinely care about solving his problem, not just making a sale. That caring showed up in my energy and presence.

The Psychological Warfare of Daily Sales Life

What Nobody Tells You About the Real Arena

You already know the field is brutal. Sales is psychological warfare—you versus doubt, exhaustion, fear, and raw rejection, every single day.

Every "not now." Every hung-up phone. Every silent email inbox sitting there, mocking you. Each one is a tiny knife, and by Thursday afternoon, you're covered in small cuts.

The fatigue creeps in after lunch. That voice in your head starts whispering: "Are you sure you're actually good enough? Maybe your luck's finally run out."

This is the real sales arena. But here's what I learned: When you approach sales as performance and entertainment—when you're genuinely excited about creating experiences for customers—the rejection stings less.

Why? Because you're focused outward on the value you're creating, not inward on your fears. You're playing a character in the best sense—not fake, but focused on serving the audience in front of you.

The Warrior Metaphor That Actually Fits

Think of yourself as a warrior marching into daily combat. Your words and your pitch are your weapons, but your shield is your mental stamina and emotional resilience.

But here's the twist: You're not a grim warrior trudging into battle. You're more like a gladiator who knows how to work the crowd. You understand that victory requires both skill and showmanship.

The top sellers wake up and actively sell themselves on their value and their mission before ever booking a single meeting. Their edge is winning the internal battle first—then bringing that confident, enthusiastic energy to every customer interaction.

Rejection: Your Secret Training Ground

The Weight Training Nobody Wants

Rejection is like daily weight training for your mental toughness. Every "no" hurts—let's not pretend it doesn't. But it builds your ability to take punches and keep swinging.

During my $50-a-week period that I mentioned in earlier chapters, rejection wasn't just painful—it was threatening to my survival. Every "no" felt personal because the stakes were so high.

But that's actually what taught me to separate my identity from my results. I had to, or I wouldn't have survived.

The sting from losing a deal doesn't signal your unworthiness. More often, it means the timing was off, your questions missed the mark, or the other side simply had different needs.

Your Rejection Log: The Secret Weapon

Some salespeople let rejection pile up until it literally buries them. The pros record it, analyze it systematically, and move on stronger.

Here's your secret weapon: Start using a rejection log. Open a notebook or digital doc and label it "Rejection Log." Record every "no"—the date, customer type, what you offered, and the actual reason they gave.

For each rejection, write a single actionable insight. Maybe your timing was off. Maybe you could have qualified better upfront. Maybe you needed more energy in your presentation.

Look for patterns weekly. Are you losing deals for the same reasons over and over?

This isn't just recordkeeping. It's systematic self-coaching so you don't bleed out from the same wound twice.

The Reframe That Changes Everything

Remember this mantra: "I am not rejected. I am redirected."

That's not empty positive thinking. It's the mental reframe that lets you turn each lost deal into a map for your next win. And here's what I added to that: Every rejection is also a performance I can improve.

Did I bring enough energy? Did I create a memorable experience? Did I layer my personality over the script effectively? These questions turn rejection into useful feedback about your craft.

Building Your Morning Mental Armor

Why the First 30 Minutes Matter

Every single day, your brain kicks off a pattern during those first waking moments. That mental groove can either hold you steady or let you drift when sales get tough.

By choosing to deliberately steer your mindset in those opening 30 minutes, you train yourself to expect progress, not setbacks (*Reframe Your Setbacks,* 2024). Instead of white-knuckling it on coffee alone, you create a ritual that becomes automatic.

The Power of Gratitude

There's a reason three items hit the sweet spot perfectly. List just one, and your mind stays on autopilot. List ten, and you're stretching just to fill space.

Three prompts you to dig in: "My client's surprising honesty yesterday." "The energy I felt after that workout." "The moment that prospect actually laughed at my joke."

Each time you drill into the "why," you wire your brain toward abundance and problem-solving for the day ahead.

Visualization That Actually Works

Close your eyes. Set a five-minute timer. Picture yourself walking into your office, feeling confident and energized. See your presentations going well. Hear the enthusiasm in your voice. Feel the handshake when the deal closes.

Engage all five senses. This isn't "thinking positive"—it's telling your body what winning feels like, so you notice opportunities and handle curveballs smoothly.

The Physical Component

Stand up and do 20 jumping jacks. Hold a power stance for two minutes. You're telling your nervous system, "Wake up, you're about to win."

Then, add your affirmation out loud: "I bring energy and value to every interaction. I create experiences that customers remember. My growth is inevitable."

Speaking creates different neural connections than thinking—turning wishful thinking into clear intent.

The Three Layers of Daily Mental Armor

- **Preparation:** Know your activity numbers for the day. Know your conversion rates. Know three strengths that set you apart—and at least one of those should be about the energy and personality you bring.

- **Perspective:** One brutal sales day is a blip. One missed quota doesn't erase months of trust and wins you've built. Write this somewhere visible: "Today is one performance, not the whole show."

- **Protection:** Create boundaries around your energy. Headphones signal focus time. A quick "I'll catch up after my calls" steers you clear of energy vampires without creating drama.

The Armor Up Visualization

Close your eyes and visualize a glowing shell around your chest that deflects harsh criticism. Picture a shield over your throat—protecting your voice and confidence. Imagine a mental filter catching negativity and letting in only useful feedback.

Hold this image for 60 seconds and repeat: "Nothing in my environment can break what I build inside" (Reeves & Whitaker, 2023).

Emotional Detachment: Building Calluses the Right Way

What Detachment Actually Means

Real emotional detachment has nothing to do with going numb. It's about developing thick enough skin so you can survive the blows without losing your drive or your compassion.

When you practice genuine emotional discipline, you start seeing the chaos of sales as outside events—not reflections of your core value.

Observe, Don't Absorb

Instead of absorbing every negative reaction as a verdict on who you are, try what elite performers do: observe, don't absorb.

Pause before you react. Picture a clear panel of glass between you and the customer. Their words hit the panel, then bounce off. Repeat silently: "I observe what's happening. I don't absorb it." Then respond logically, not emotionally.

This takes practice, but every time you manage to keep your center, you retrain your mind. The feedback loop that usually amplifies stress loses its fuel.

Separating "You" From Your Results

The Identity Trap

Too many salespeople tie their identity to their numbers. Your numbers go up, and you feel unstoppable. Then you slip, and your confidence plummets.

This dangerous connection becomes a devastating feedback loop. Motivation swings wildly with every outcome.

The Escape Route

Results are outcomes, not definitions of who you are. Instead of saying, "I failed," try, "That tactic didn't work this time." Instead of, "I'm not good at this," try, "I'm still learning this skill."

Value yourself for the effort you put in consistently. Value yourself for the energy and personality you bring to every interaction. Value yourself for your commitment to creating memorable customer experiences.

Your new mantra: "My worth is intrinsic, not conditional."

The Mirror Rule: Building Unshakeable Self-Worth

What Real Confidence Looks Like

Healthy pride means you know what you're good at and you respect your ability—but you don't feel the need to prove it at everyone else's expense.

Your customers feel this difference instantly. When you show pride grounded in quiet competence, you invite trust.

The Mirror Rule

Every morning, look yourself directly in the eyes and say: "I am the best version of myself today—and that's enough. I bring energy, personality, and genuine value to every interaction."

Don't rush through it. Meet your own gaze until you believe it. This tells your brain that you set your own value (Cascio et al., 2015).

How This Changes Your Sales Approach

When you show up from this grounded place, customers respond to your confidence more powerfully than any product spec.

State your price firmly and then stop talking. Share your expertise without launching into an aggressive hard sell. Trust that you know your stuff—and that you bring something special to the table through your energy and personality.

Turning "No" Into Fuel: The Numbers Game Reframe

The Statistical Reality

Every "no" is statistical proof that you're one step closer to a "yes." If one in ten prospects converts, then each rejection is literally another milepost toward your next winner.

The 30-Day No Tracking Challenge

For 30 days, keep a log of every rejection. But instead of tallying wounds, celebrate each one as proof that you're putting in the reps. You're in the game, not watching from the sidelines.

You'll notice patterns—certain times when prospects are more receptive, specific approaches that work better, particular moments when your energy made the difference.

A Personal Story

From my own journey: I once had an 18-call streak of flat turn-downs. Every single call ended with "not interested."

But call number 19 changed everything. The company on the other end, after hearing my pitch and sensing my unwavering enthusiasm (which came from surviving so much rejection), signed up for a partnership that doubled my previous best commission.

The breakthrough came not despite the rejection, but because relentless follow-through made me genuinely unstoppable.

Learning From Loss: The Three R's Method

Why Losing Only Hurts if You Refuse to Learn

After a failed presentation, step away briefly and then ask honestly: *What derailed this? Where could I have brought more energy? Did I create a memorable experience or just deliver information?*

Treat the loss as paid tuition for your sales education. Review the details without brutal self-scolding.

The Three R's Method

1. **Record:** Write exactly what happened, sticking to observable facts.

2. **Reflect:** Identify what worked and what didn't. Ask: "Did my energy level affect the outcome? Did I entertain while informing? Did I layer personality over the script effectively?"

3. **Reframe:** Turn each misstep into one specific thing you'll try differently next time.

The mantra: "There's no such thing as losing—only learning faster than the next person" (Growth Mindset Flashcards, 2025).

Creating a Customer Experience Instead of a Pitch

The Fundamental Shift

Here's the ultimate realization I came to: Every interaction is either a transaction or an experience. Transactions are forgettable. Experiences create loyalty, referrals, and long-term relationships.

When I shifted from "making pitches" to "creating experiences," everything changed. Customers stopped seeing me as just another salesperson trying to get their money. They saw me as someone who brought value, energy, and even enjoyment to their day.

The Performance Mindset

Think about the best presentations, speeches, or performances you've ever witnessed. They weren't just informative—they were engaging, memorable, and emotional.

That's what your sales interactions should feel like. Not manipulative or fake, but genuinely engaging. You're not just transferring information—you're creating a moment that matters.

I started treating every presentation like a performance. That meant rehearsing, yes, but also bringing spontaneity and responsiveness. It meant reading the room and adjusting my energy. It meant using humor, storytelling, and demonstration to keep people engaged.

Why This Matters More Than Ever

In a world where customers can research products online and compare features in seconds, what sets you apart isn't your product knowledge. It's the experience you create.

Customers might forget your features. They'll remember how you made them feel. They'll remember if you brought energy, personality, and genuine enthusiasm. They'll remember if you entertained while you educated.

Wrapping It Up

As I learned during my journey from $50 a week to building a thriving customer base, mental toughness isn't just about surviving. It's about showing up with so much confidence, energy, and personality that customers can't help but be drawn in.

Keep showing up for yourself each morning with intention. Bring your whole personality to every interaction. Create experiences, not just pitches. Turn product features into performances. Make every customer interaction memorable.

This mindset shift doesn't just help you close more deals—though it will. It shapes you into a relentless, unstoppable force who creates value, builds relationships, and succeeds again and again.

So, gear up. Bring your energy. Create experiences worth remembering. And get ready to own your sales journey like never before.

Conclusion:
The Million-Dollar Mindset—Your Sales Legacy Starts Today

When I stood on top of that desk in a chaotic timeshare boiler room, shouting my pitch louder than everyone around me, I had no idea I was beginning a journey that would take me from $50 a week to selling over $50 million. I didn't know that crawling under my desk just to hear customers would teach me about adaptation and problem-solving. I couldn't have imagined that the kid with no sales experience, standing on furniture like a crazy person, would one day write a book to help others discover their own potential.

But here's what I've learned after three decades in sales: Your starting point doesn't determine your destination. Your circumstances don't define your capabilities. And your past doesn't limit your future.

The Real Secret

Throughout this book, we've covered everything from mastering cold calls to developing mental toughness, from handling objections to becoming a leader. We've explored voice techniques, body language, goal-setting, and the psychology of closing. But if there's one truth that ties everything together, it's this: Sales success isn't about what you do—it's about who you become.

The techniques matter. The fundamentals are essential. The strategies work. But what separates the $50-a-week salesperson from the million-dollar producer isn't just skill—it's mindset, character, and an unwavering commitment to growth.

When my mentor told me, "The pat on the back is your own paycheck," he wasn't just talking about commission. He was talking about ownership—taking complete responsibility for your results, your development, and your future. When he said, "Act like a lifer," he was teaching me that excellence requires total commitment, not one foot out the door looking for something easier.

What You've Gained

If you've made it this far, you're not the same person who started Chapter 1. You now possess:

a proven framework for building authentic connections and closing deals

the tools to transform objections into opportunities and rejection into fuel

the mindset to project confidence, resilience, and leadership

the knowledge that you already have everything you need to succeed

You've learned that cold calling is a numbers game combined with emotional intelligence. That your voice carries more weight than your words. That objections are simply requests for more information. That closing is about assumption, not pressure. And most importantly, that becoming a leader—whether of yourself or others—is the ultimate sales skill.

The Path Forward

Your journey doesn't end here; it accelerates after what you've learned. Every call you make, every objection you handle, every goal you set, and every setback you overcome is building something bigger than a sales career. You're building a legacy.

Remember these truths as you move forward:

- **Don't give up before the miracle happens:** I almost quit after those $50 weeks. Most people would have. But I refused to accept that result and committed to figuring out how to earn more. That decision changed everything.

- **You can't have one foot out the door and expect to excel:** When you have nothing to fall back on, you find a way forward. When you act like this is all you have, you become the best at what you do.

- **Every "no" brings you closer to a "yes":** Those hang-ups that felt personal? They were just stepping stones. That rejection that stung? It was teaching you resilience. The path isn't smooth, but it's worth walking.

- **Absorb everything like a sponge:** Develop a mindset of learning everything about your job, your industry, and your customers. The salesperson who stops learning stops growing.

- **To keep it, you have to give it away:** True leadership means empowering others, sharing knowledge, and lifting people up. The more you give, the more you receive.

Your Defining Moment

Remember that timeshare room at the beginning of this book? That moment when I stood on my desk, got louder than everyone else, and watched my appointment numbers skyrocket? That wasn't just about volume; it was about finding the courage to do what others wouldn't, to stand out when it felt uncomfortable, to turn energy and excitement into results.

You've had your own version of that moment, or you're about to. Maybe it's your first closed deal. Maybe it's the day you realize rejection doesn't hurt anymore. Maybe it's when someone asks you to mentor them because they see something in you worth learning from.

Whatever your moment is, recognize it. Celebrate it. Then use it as fuel to keep going.

The Question That Changes Everything

I was told I was going to be someone special when I grew up. Those words stayed with me through rough beginnings, working entry-level jobs, and making $50 a week. They stayed with me through thousands of cold calls, countless rejections, and every moment I wanted to quit.

Now, I'm passing those words to you: You are going to be someone special.

Not because of some magical "sales gene." Not because the path will be easy. But because you've picked up this book, absorbed these lessons, and made a decision to become more than you were yesterday.

The only question left is: What will you do with what you now know?

Your Legacy Awaits

The transformation from timeshare phones to boardrooms isn't about geography—it's about growth. It's about the person with no experience who stood on a desk and refused to blend in. It's about the salesperson making $50 a week who decided that wasn't acceptable. It's about you, right now, choosing to step into the sales professional you're meant to become.

You have the tools. You have the framework. You have the mindset. Most importantly, you have the courage—because you've already taken the first step by reading this book.

Now, it's time to take the next step. And the one after that. And the one after that.

Your sales journey doesn't begin when everything feels perfect. It begins the moment you decide to start.

So, make your first call. Handle that objection. Set that ambitious goal. Project that confidence. Become that leader.

The boardroom isn't some distant destination; it's wherever you decide to show up with excellence, authenticity, and unwavering commitment.

Your defining moment is waiting. Go create it.

References

11 Buying signals to look out for (verbal & nonverbal). (n.d.). *Qwilr*. https://qwilr.com/blog/sales-buying-signals/

Academy, S. (2025, February 28). *Unlock your best speaking voice*. SHELBY Academy. https://shelbyacademy.org/unlock-your-best-speaking-voice/

Affirmations - anxiety skill building | Wayfinder Wellness. (2025). *Talk with Wayfinder*. https://www.talkwithwayfinder.com/skills/affirmations

Asian Institute of Management. (2025, July 27). *Asian Institute of Management*. https://aim.edu/programs/sales-manager-leadership-development/

Avoiding hang-ups: Cold call opener essentials. (2025). *ZoomInfo Blog*. https://pipeline.zoominfo.com/sales/avoiding-hang-ups-cold-call-opener-essentials

BevNET Live L.A. 2025. (2025). *BevNET*. http://www.bevnet.com/events/bevnetlive

Bordo, S., Costanzo, G., & Villani, D. (2025, May 21). Enhancing psychological skills and well-being in sport through an app-based blended intervention: A randomized controlled pilot study. *BMC Psychology*. https://doi.org/10.1186/s40359-025-02824-8

Bloomenthal, A. (2024). *Value-based pricing*. Investopedia. https://www.investopedia.com/terms/v/valuebasedpricing.asp

Cabuyao, K. (2023, October 11). The importance of self-awareness in becoming better leaders. *IHF*. http://ihf-fih.org/news-insights/the-importance-of-self-awareness-in-becoming-better-leaders/

Carrier, J. (2019, July 4). Mehrabian's 7-38-55 communication model: It's more than words. *PeopleShift*. https://people-shift.com/articles/mehrabians-7-38-55-communication-model/

Cascio, C. N., O'Donnell, M. B., Tinney, F. J., Lieberman, M. D., Taylor, S. E., Strecher, V. J., & Falk, E. B. (2015, November 5). Self-affirmation activates brain systems associated with self-related processing and reward and is reinforced by future orientation. *Social Cognitive and Affective Neuroscience*. https://doi.org/10.1093/scan/nsv136

Chandrasekara, A. (2023, September 11). The power of repetition: Mastering skills through consistency. *Medium*. https://ashanchandrasekara.medium.com/the-power-of-repetition-mastering-skills-through-consistency-6ac2b417ead3

Confidence vs arrogance: The fine line that changes everything. (2025). *The Power Ark*. https://thepowerark.com/articles/confidence-vs-arrogance-fine-line-changes-everything

Corona, A. (2025, January 6). Mastering assertiveness: How to boost confidence and build stronger client relationships. *FreelanceLatam*. https://freelancelatam.com/assertiveness-in-you-and-your-work/

Cuncic, A. (2024, February 12). 7 active listening techniques for better communication. *Verywell Mind*. https://www.verywellmind.com/what-is-active-listening-3024343

DeCastro, M. (2020, March 19). 12 mindful selling attributes of top performing sales professionals. *Medium*. https://mauricedecastro.medium.com/12-mindful-selling-attributes-of-top-performing-sales-professionals-a21883919fd5

Deel. (n.d.). *Employee potential*. https://www.deel.com/glossary/employee-potential/

Developing mission, vision, and values. (n.d.). *2012books.lardbucket.org*. https://2012books.lardbucket.org/books/management-principles-v1.0/s08-developing-mission-vision-and-.html

Difficult conversations — Improve your leadership skills. (2023, July 24). *Bruce Mayhew Consulting.* https://www.brucemayhewconsulting.com/blog/category/Difficult+Conversations

DSpace. (2025). *Iowa State University.* https://dr.lib.iastate.edu/bitstreams/3a746742-9415-4132-b892-0d8724764470/download

Followership: The Cinderella of leadership. (2025). *Alina Florea.* https://www.alinaflorea.net/newsletter-57-june-2024

Frost, A. (2023, April 19). The ultimate guide to sales metrics. *HubSpot.* https://blog.hubspot.com/sales/sales-metrics

García-Monge, A., Guijarro-Romero, S., Santamaría-Vázquez, E., Martínez-Álvarez, L., & Bores-Calle, N. (2023). Embodied strategies for public speaking anxiety. *Frontiers in Human Neuroscience.* https://doi.org/10.3389/fnhum.2023.1268798

Georgeson, Z. (2024, February 22). Consider performance targets for setting executive incentive goals. *WTW.* https://www.wtwco.com/en-ca/insights/2024/02/consider-performance-targets-for-setting-executive-incentive-goals

Gibbons, S. (2018, June 19). You and your business have 7 seconds to make a first impression: Here's how to succeed. *Forbes.* https://www.forbes.com/sites/serenitygibbons/2018/06/19/you-have-7-seconds-to-make-a-first-impression-heres-how-to-succeed/

Gibson, K. (2024, January 23). Why identifying your target audience is important. *Harvard Business School.* https://online.hbs.edu/blog/post/target-audience-in-marketing

Growth mindset flashcards. (2025). *Quizlet.* https://quizlet.com/1069295090/growth-mindset-flash-cards/

Guler, U. D. (2025, March 3). Build perfect customer personas with example templates. *Tabular.* https://tabular.email/blog/what-is-a-customer-persona

Hazy, J. K., & Boyatzis, R. E. (2015, June 12). Emotional contagion and proto-organizing in human interaction dynamics. *Frontiers in Psychology*. https://doi.org/10.3389/fpsyg.2015.00806

Hoek, K., Suur, L., van Velzen, M., & Sarton, E. Y. (2025, June 12). Implementation and evaluation of a therapeutic communication educational program. *JMIR Research Protocols*. https://doi.org/10.2196/65795

Intelemark. (2025, April 11). 8 techniques to minimize hang-ups and enhance telemarketing engagement. https://www.intelemark.com/blog/8-techniques-to-minimize-hang-ups-and-enhance-telemarketing-engagement/

Linton, E. (2023). Employee expectations from leadership (2023). *Digital Defynd*. https://digitaldefynd.com/IQ/employee-expectations-from-leadership/

Moore, W. (2025, October 31). How to be yourself: 7 science-backed steps to stop people-pleasing. *MooreMomentum*. https://mooremomentum.com/blog/how-to-be-yourself-in-a-world-that-wants-you-to-be-someone-else/

Noor, T. (2022). Navigating burnout in modern workplaces. *Harvard Business Review*. https://hbr.org/2022/07/navigating-burnout-in-modern-workplaces

PwC. (2023). *Global workforce hopes and fears survey 2023*. https://www.pwc.com/gx/en/issues/workforce/hopes-and-fears.html

Reeves, M., & Whitaker, K. (2023). *Resilient organizations: A roadmap for sustained performance*. Boston Consulting Group. https://www.bcg.com/publications/2023/resilient-organizations-roadmap-for-sustained-performance

Reframe your setbacks: Turning challenges into learning opportunities. (2024, September 18). *My Health for Life*. https://www.myhealthforlife.com.au/news/reframe-your-setbacks/

Robinson, L. (2024). Why employees leave: The overlooked drivers of turnover. *SHRM*. https://www.shrm.org/resourcesandtools/hr-topics/employee-relations/pages/why-employees-leave-overlooked-drivers-turnover.aspx

Russell, H. (2023, May 17). Phone call anxiety: Simple ways to overcome your telephobia, according to psychology. *BBC Science Focus Magazine*. https://www.sciencefocus.com/the-human-body/telephobia

Soni, A. (2025, November 3). Micro expressions: The silent language of human emotions. *PlanetSpark*. https://www.planetspark.in/communication-skills/micro-expressions-the-silent-language-of-emotions/

Team AASC. (2025, March 12). Healthy mind, healthy body: The importance of mental health in physical wellness. *AASC Spine*. https://www.aascspine.com/blog/healthy-mind-healthy-body-the-importance-of-mental-health-in-physical-wellness

The Power of Putting Pen to Paper: How writing down goals transforms dreams into reality. (2024, April 16). *UPM Communication Papers*. https://www.upmpaper.com/knowledge-inspiration/blog-stories/articles/2024/the-power-of-putting-pen-to-paper/

The Psychology of Urgency: 9 ways to drive conversions. (2018, June 26). *Smart Insights*. https://www.smartinsights.com/digital-marketing-strategy/psychology-urgency-9-ways-drive-conversions/

Training Magazine. (n.d.). *How to build stronger relationships at work*. https://trainingmag.com/how-to-build-stronger-relationships-at-work/

Vaish, A., Grossmann, T., & Woodward, A. (2008). Not all emotions are created equal: The negativity bias in social-emotional development. *PLoS ONE, 3*(7), e3668. https://doi.org/10.1371/journal.pone.0003668

Wolf, P. (2025, November 24). LAER model in customer success: How to use it for efficiency. *Custify.* https://www.custify.com/blog/laer-model/